HENN 2016

Jahrbuch

Inhalt

Content

rt

Wir kommunizieren Architektur - so auch in diesem Jahrbuch - hauptsächlich visuell. Der eigentliche Wert und die spezifische Leistung von Architektur liegen aber nicht in ihrem Bild, sondern in ihrer räumlichen Ordnung. Das Raumsystem führt uns zusammen und trennt uns, führt uns zu einem Ort und wieder zurück, schließt uns ein oder aus. Es scheint kaum eine Ordnung in unserer Gesellschaft lesbarer zu sein als die räumliche Ordnung, wie Dirk Baecker schreibt. Dabei nehmen wir den Raum nicht als ein Gegenüber wahr, wie ein Objekt oder ein Bild, sondern wir sind im Raum, wir werden beeinflusst, und wir beeinflussen.

Begriffe wie Perspektivenvielfalt, Innovation oder Inklusion weisen darauf hin, dass sich die Gesellschaft tiefgreifend verändert. Mit ihr verändern sich auch die Arbeitswelten, dafür stehen Themen wie Industrie 4.0, Smart Working oder Corporate Culture. Als Architekt muss man sich die Frage stellen, ob die konventionellen Raumstrukturen diesen Entwicklungen noch entsprechen. Es fällt auf, dass die Arbeit

We communicate architecture – as in this yearbook – primarily in a visual way. The actual value and the specific performance of architecture, however, are not replicated in their image but in their spatial order. The spatial system brings us together and separates us, leads us to a place and brings us back, closes us in or out. As Dirk Baecker wrote, there seems to be hardly any order in our society that is more legible than spatial order, whereby we do not perceive space face to face like an object or a picture, but find ourselves in a space – we are being influenced and we are influencing.

Terms such as richness of perspective, innovation or inclusion are indications that society is undergoing radical changes which are accompanied by changes in the working environment with themes such as Industry 4.0, Smart Working and Corporate Culture. An architect must consider whether conventional spatial arrangements are still of relevance to these developments. It is apparent that work can no longer be fully divided into functions which

Vorwo

nicht mehr restlos in Funktionen aufteilbar ist, denen man Räume zuweisen könnte. Ein maßgeblicher Teil der Arbeit besteht heute in einem kommunikativen Prozess, der zwischen den etablierten Funktionen entsteht. Die bisherigen Funktionen werden nicht mehr organisatorisch verbunden, sondern kommunikativ gekoppelt. Wie man diese Kommunikationsprozesse in einer architektonischen Ordnung gestaltet, ist die eigentliche Herausforderung und die neue Aufgabe.

Der Gesamtprozess in Unternehmen und Organisationen entsteht nicht mehr durch Planung und Anweisung, sondern durch Kommunikation. Heute verbindet die Kommunikation alles miteinander. Darin drückt sich keine Beliebigkeit aus, sondern eine neue soziale Ordnungsform. Diese gesellschaftliche Form wird erst sichtbar in den Folgerungen, die die Architektur daraus zieht. Innovation z.B. entsteht durch interdisziplinäre Kooperation. Interdisziplinarität ist keine weitere Disziplin, sondern verbindet die einzelnen Disziplinen. Architektur hat die Aufgabe, dies im Medium des Raumes

could be allocated to a certain space. A major part of work today consists of a communicative process evolving between the established functions. The previous functions are no longer connected organisationally but are communicatively coupled. The real challenge and new task is to find a way of absorbing these communication processes into an architectural order.

The overall processes in companies and organisations are no longer shaped by planning and instruction, but through communication. Today communication binds everything together. This, however, is not an expression of arbitrariness but of a new form of social order. This societal form only becomes visible through the conclusions which architecture draws from it. Innovation, for example, develops through interdisciplinary cooperation. Multidisciplinarity is not an additional discipline; it connects the individual disciplines and it is the task of architecture to express this through the medium of space. The disciplines will therefore no longer be connected by

auszudrücken. Die Disziplinen werden dann nicht mehr durch Flure erschlossen, sondern durch einen Kommunikationsraum verbunden. Umgekehrt bedeutet das: Der Raum der interdisziplinären Kommunikation wird nicht einfach an die disziplinären Räume angehängt, sondern er muss von ihnen „unterschieden" werden.

Diese Unterscheidungen sind zunächst rein gedanklich. Beim Entwerfen und Planen von Gebäuden geht es schlussendlich darum, die Raumstruktur wahrnehmbar und benutzbar und für das Erleben und Handeln der Menschen relevant zu machen. Nur dann kann sie Teil einer neuen sozialen Ordnung werden. Hier greifen die klassischen Disziplinen der Architektur, also Formgebung und Proportion, Konstruktion und Detaillierung, Material und Farbe.

Das Ergebnis kann dann so aussehen, dass die disziplinären Räume sich in Boxen befinden, die von einem interdisziplinären Kontinuum umhüllt werden.

corridors but by communication space. Conversely, this means that the space for interdisciplinary communication will not simply be attached to the disciplinary space, but must be "distinguished" from them.

Initially these distinctions are merely theoretical. Ultimately, when designing and planning buildings, the spatial structure must be perceptible as well as useable and made relevant to the experience and actions of people. Only then can this be a part of the new social order. This is where the traditional architectural disciplines such as design and proportion, construction and detailing, material and colour, take hold.

The result may be such that the disciplinary spaces appear to be boxes encapsulated in a multidisciplinary continuum. It may be that they have direct visual connection and immediate access to an atrium. An interdisciplinary space can also be a central area in which current work results can be seen from everywhere – or an accessible, sculptural linking of all

Es kann sein, dass sie unmittelbare Verbindung mit einem Atrium haben. Ein interdisziplinärer Raum kann auch ein zentraler Raum sein, in dem das aktuelle Arbeitsergebnis von überall her gesehen wird - oder eine begehbare, skulpturale Verbindung aller Gebäudeebenen, die das Erlebnis vermittelt, an jedem Punkt im ganzen Haus zu sein. Der Raum der Kommunikation kann auch eine Magistrale sein, die alles in Bewegung miteinander verbindet. Es ist ein notwendiger Schritt in jedem Projekt, die spezifische Raumstruktur zu entwickeln.

Insgesamt deutet sich dabei eine neue Gebäudetypologie an. In ihren Raumstrukturen werden die neuen gesellschaftlichen Ordnungen leichter lesbar - und lebbar.

Gunter Henn

building levels, communicating the experience of being at every point of the building. The communication space can also be a central axis, connecting everything in motion.

Indications of a new building typology are emerging. With their spatial design, the new societal orders will be more legible – and liveable.

zaland

Zalando Headquarters

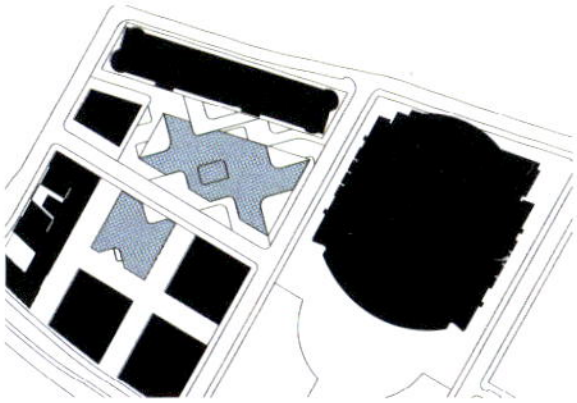

Zalando
Berlin
2015 – 2018

Technische Ausrüstung
BuroHappold, Berlin
Brandschutz
hhpberlin, Berlin
Bauphysik
Müller-BBM, Planegg
Innenraumkonzept
KINZO, Berlin
Lichtplaner
Bartenbach LichtLabor, A-Aldrans

Wettbewerb 2015
1. Preis

Competition 2015
1st Prize

Das neue Zalando Hauptquartier ist als Ensemble aus zwei Neubauten geplant, die das Herzstück des Unternehmenscampus am neuen Standort in Berlin-Friedrichshain bilden. Das Projekt sieht zwei siebengeschossige Volumen mit insgesamt rund 42.000 m² Bürofläche vor. Hier sollen in Zukunft bis zu 2.700 Mitarbeiter von Europas größtem Online-Anbieter für Schuhe und Fashion arbeiten.
Die Gebäudegrundrisse verschieben die Rasterstruktur der Blockrandbebauung diagonal zum Bebauungsplan. Die Innenhöfe werden dadurch an die Grundstücksaußenkanten gerückt. Durch diese Öffnung entstehen Übergänge zwischen den Büros und dem öffentlichen Raum. Weitere Ein- und Ausblicke gewähren die transparenten und transluzenten Fassaden, welche die Vielfalt des Unternehmens nach Außen wirken lassen.
Das vertikale Atrium im Hauptgebäude öffnet sich mit einem Luftraum über die gesamte Gebäudehöhe. Die zentrale Lobby wird von einer Treppe mit Sitz- und Loungebereichen flankiert, die auch für Veranstaltungen genutzt werden kann.

The new Zalando Headquarters' a duo of buildings designed to form the heart of the corporate campus at the new site in Berlin-Friedrichshain. The project's two seven-storey buildings provide some 42,000 m² of office space. Up to 2,700 employees will work here for Europe's largest online supplier of shoes and fashion goods.
The plan layout rotates the building grid diagonally to the development plan thus placing the internal courtyards at the outer edges of the plot. This opening creates transitions between office and public space. Further views into and out of the building are ensured by transparent and translucent façades that express the diversity of the company to the world outside.
The vertical atrium in the main building opens into a space that extends to the full height of the building. The central lobby is flanked by a bank of steps with seating and lounge areas, which can also be used for exhibitions and similar events. The auditorium and the conference and training zones connect to a café and the company restaurant.

Der neue Zalando Campus (1) an der Spree zwischen Ostbahnhof (2) und Warschauer Straße (3).

The new Zalando Campus (1) on the Spree River between Ostbahnhof (2) and Warschauer Street (3).

Berliner Block Hoftypologie
Berlin Block Courtyard typology

→

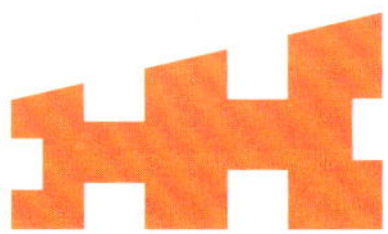

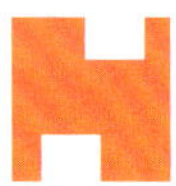

Bürogebäude Einschnitte
Office building with recesses

→

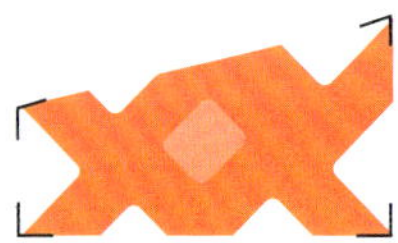

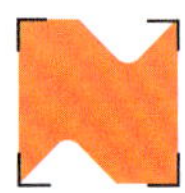

Headquarter Zalando

Berliner Block anders gedacht: Zalando ist ein Berliner Unternehmen, das anders denkt und unbekannte Wege geht - es erfindet sich jeden Tag neu, auch den Berliner Blockrand.

Rethinking the Berlin Block: Zalando is a Berlin company that thinks differently and that enters new, unknown paths - it reinvents not only itself constantly, but also reinterpretates the typology of the Berlin Block.

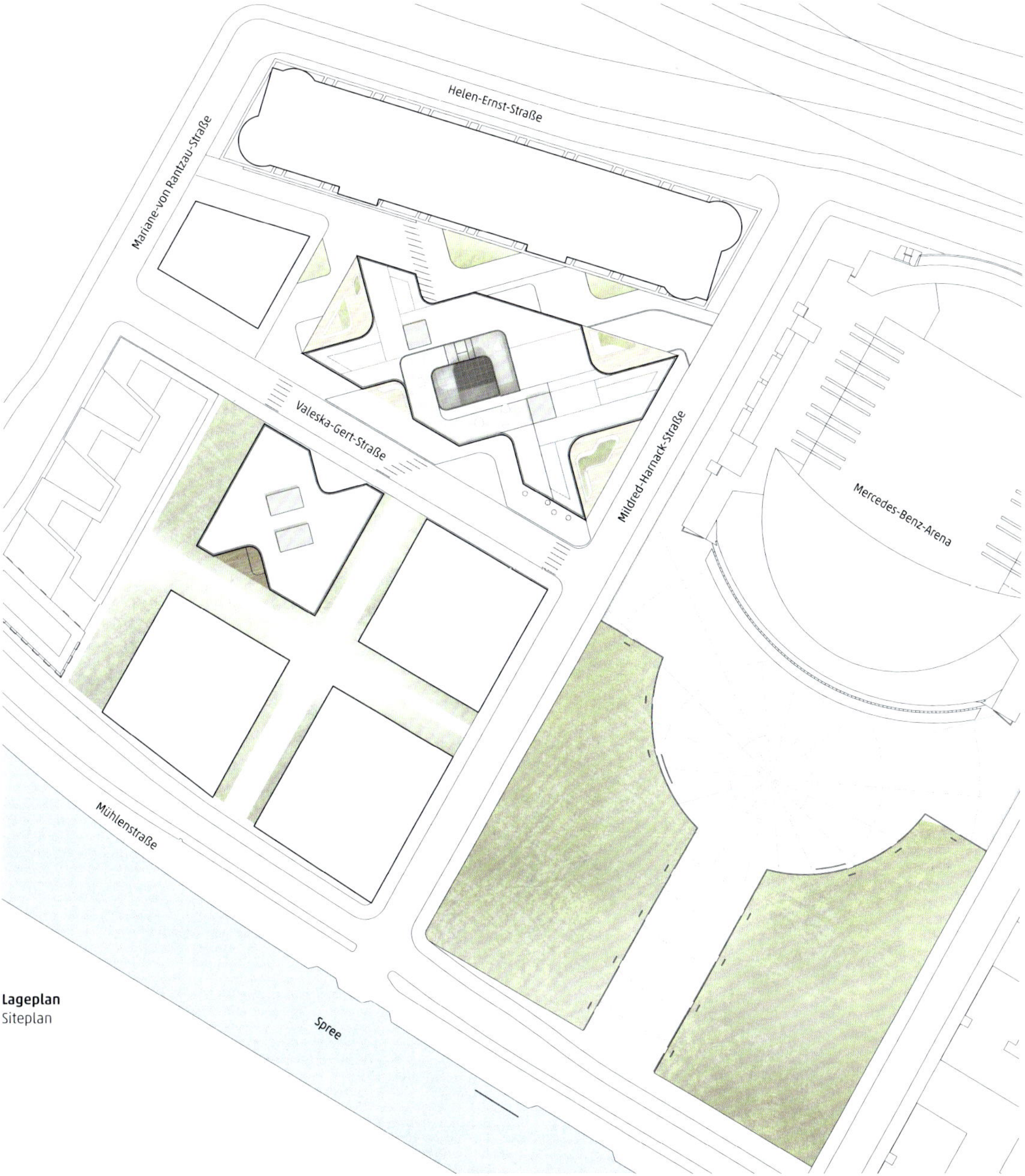

Lageplan
Siteplan

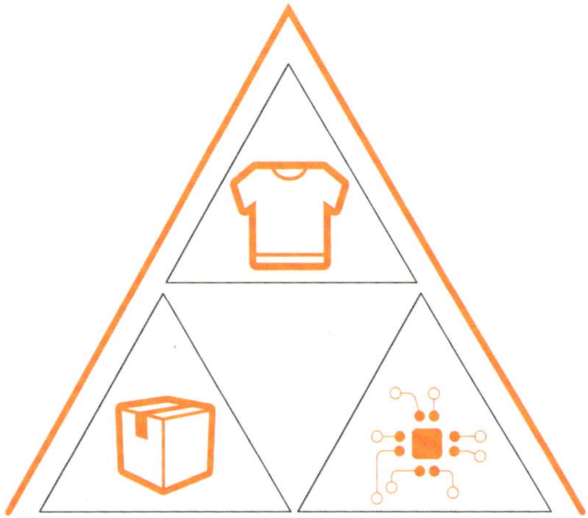

Drei starke Identitäten unter einem Dach vereint
Three strong identities under one roof

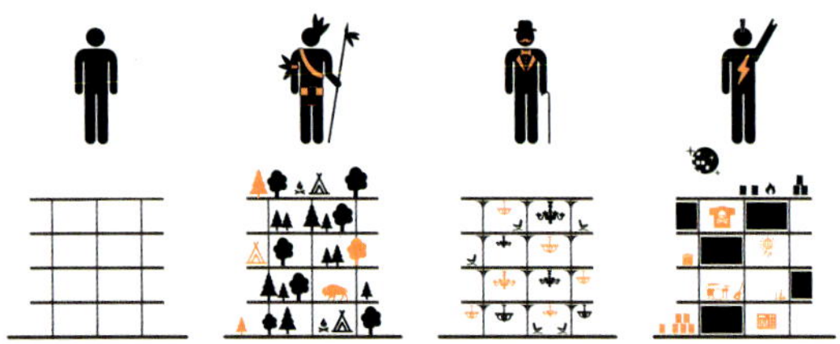

Das Gebäude besetzen und zu Eigen machen
Occupy the house and make it your own

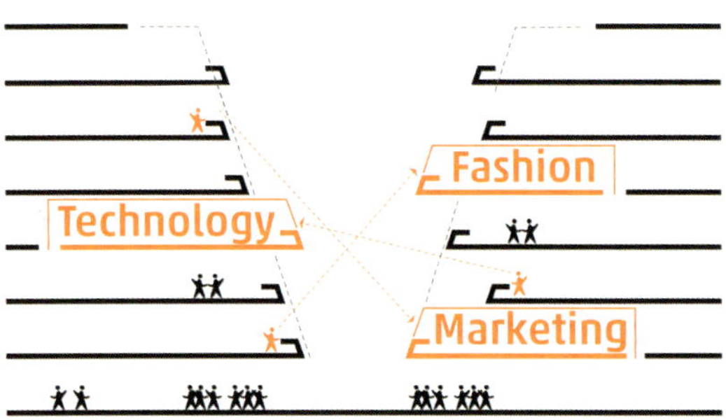

Awareness – Identitäten sichtbar machen
Awareness – identities become visible

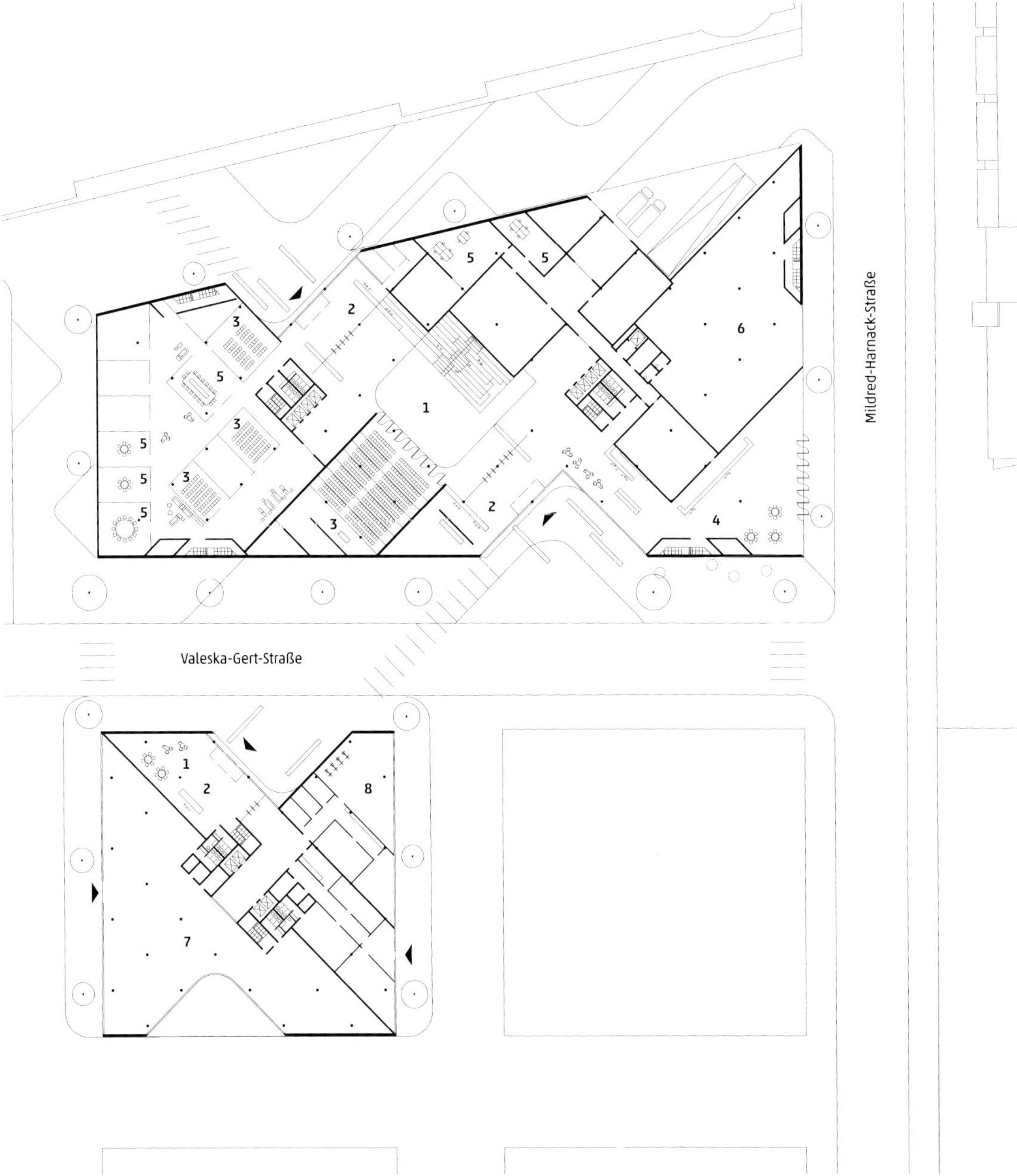
Mildred-Harnack-Straße
Valeska-Gert-Straße
1
2
3
4
5
6
7
8

Schnitt durch das Atrium mit Foyer und Auditorium

Cross section through the atrium with foyer and auditorium

Das Auditorium sowie Konferenz- und Schulungszonen schließen sich neben einem Café und der Kantine daran an. Die räumliche Organisation der Büros in den Obergeschossen geht mit Konzentrations- als auch Interaktionszonen auf die wechselnden Bedürfnisse der Mitarbeiter ein und ermöglicht differenzierte Nutzungen. Rund um das Atrium sind Sonderflächen für den sozialen Austausch gruppiert. Freitreppen verkürzen die Wege zwischen diesen Gemeinschaftsbereichen in den einzelnen Geschossen. Die Arbeitszonen selbst passen sich flexibel an wechselnde Teamgrößen an. Zentrale Bereiche für die Projektarbeit sind mittig platziert. Von ihnen ausgehend verwandelt sich die Arbeitsatmosphäre der weiteren Nutzungsbereiche graduell bis hin zu ruhigen Konzentrations- und Rückzugszonen für jeden Einzelnen. Sogenannte Catwalks verbinden die einzelnen Neighbourhoods, sie erlauben informelle Meetings und verstärken den multidisziplinären Charakter des Arbeitsalltags bei Zalando.

The spatial organisation of the office with separate zones for work requiring intensive concentration and interaction on the above-ground floors specifically caters for the changing requirements of the employees and offers differentiated use options. Special areas for social interaction are grouped around the atrium. Open stairways shorten the routes between these common areas on individual floors. The work zones can be flexibly reconfigured for changing team sizes. The main areas for project work are located centrally. From there, the working atmosphere of other use areas gradually changes to peaceful concentration and withdrawal zones to suit everyone. "Catwalks" connect the individual neighbourhoods, allowing space for informal meetings and strengthening the multidisciplinary character of the working day at Zalando.

Erdgeschoss

1 Lobby
2 Rezeption
3 Auditorium
4 Foodcourt
5 Meetingräume
6 Kollektionslager
7 Kita
8 Sport

Ground level

1 Lobby
2 Reception
3 Auditorium
4 Foodcourt
5 Meeting rooms
6 Collection storage
7 Day care centre
8 Exercise room

1. Obergeschoss	First floor
1 Showroom	1 Showroom
2 Living room	2 Living room
3 Terrassen	3 Terraces
4 Arbeitsplätze	4 Workplaces
5 Meetingräume	5 Meeting rooms
6 Projekträume	6 Project rooms
7 Teeküche	7 Coffee point

WESTWOOD
COLLECTION STORAGE

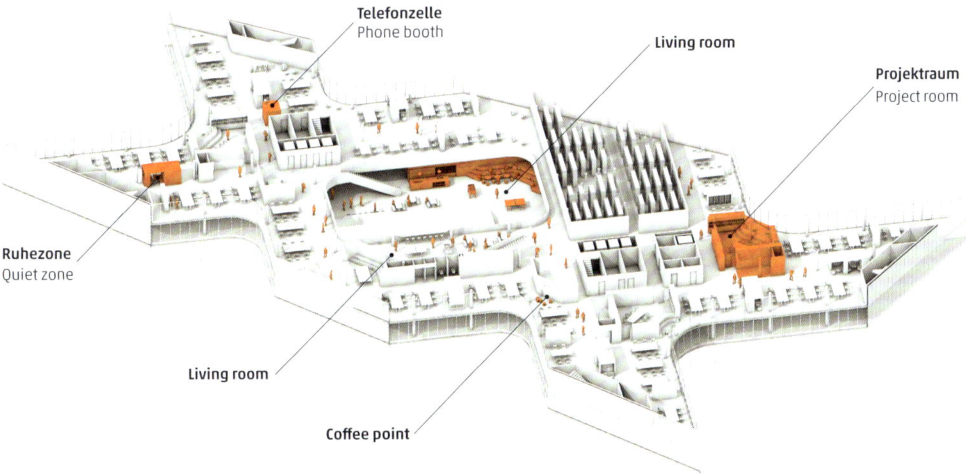
Telefonzelle
Phone booth
Living room
Projektraum
Project room
Ruhezone
Quiet zone
Living room
Coffee point

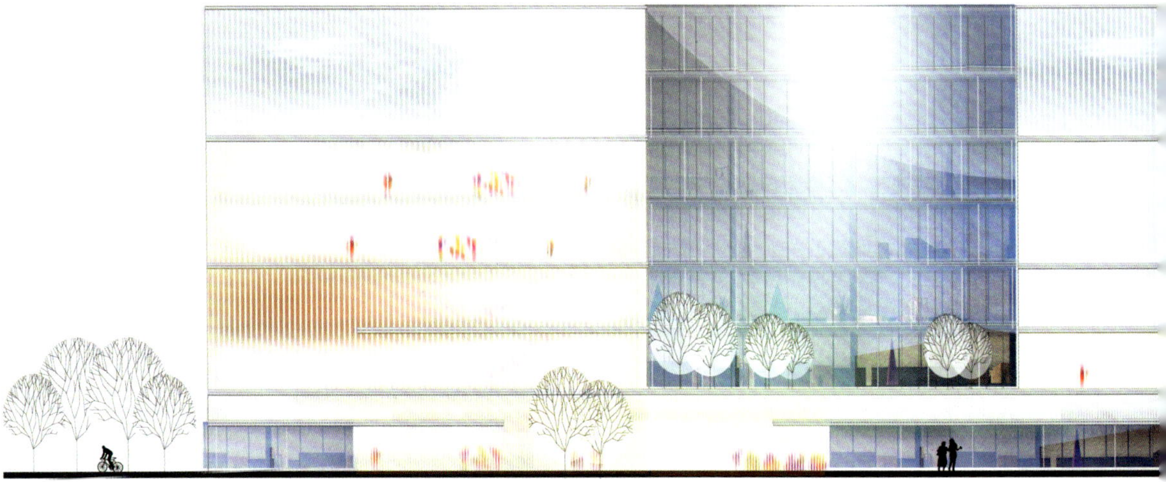

Wechselspiel von transparenten und transluzenten Fassaden

Interplay with alternating transparent and translucent façades

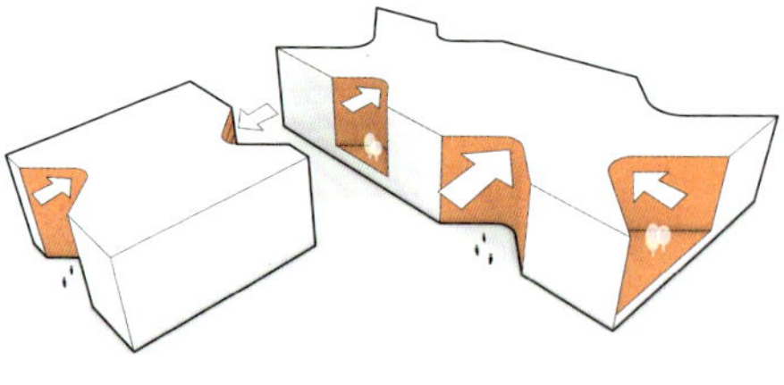

Hauptfassade mit Eingang von der Valeska-Gert-Straße

Main façade with entrance at Valeska-Gert Street

HVB-Tower Modernisierung Eingangshalle

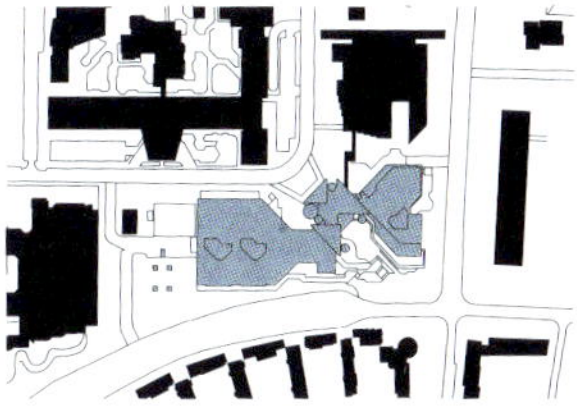

HVZ GmbH & Co. Objekt KG, München
2011 – 2016

Architekt, 1981
Walther und Bea Betz, München

Technische Ausrüstung
Climaplan, München
Tragwerksplaner
bwp Burggraf + Reiminger, München
Bauphysik
Müller-BBM, Planegg
Brandschutz
a+p Architekten, München
Elektrotechnik
Ingenieurbüro Knab, München
Fassadenplaner
R+R Fuchs, München
Lichtplaner
Schmidt König, München
Vermessung
GT Ziegler, München

Das Hochhaus der Hypovereinsbank am Münchner Arabellapark wird von Grund auf umfassend saniert. Ein wesentliches Ziel dabei ist die erhebliche Reduzierung des Energieverbrauchs und des daran gekoppelten CO_2-Ausstoßes des Gebäudes. Nach seiner Sanierung soll der 27-geschossige Turm von 1981, der als erstes Gebäude in München die 100-Meter-Marke überragte, als Green Building zertifiziert werden. Um den einzigartigen optischen Charakter des denkmalgeschützten HVB-Towers zu wahren, wird die Ertüchtigung seiner Fassade nach innen aufgebaut.
Die Innenräume des Hochhauses werden entkernt, als flexible sowie zukunftsfähige Smart Working-Büros neu interpretiert und an die herausragende gestalterische Qualität des äußeren Erscheinungsbildes angeglichen. Das Erschließungsbauwerk des Flachbaus, über dem der Turm schwebt, erhält ein neu gestaltetes Foyer, das der zukünftigen Nutzung als Vorstandssitz gerecht wird. In seinem Zentrum erstreckt sich vom Erdgeschoss über zwei Etagen ein spektakulär gefalteter Raum nach oben. Durch polygonale Flächen, die sich in unter-

The Hypovereinsbank high-rise building in Arabellapark in Munich is to be extensively redeveloped. One of the main objectives is to substantially reduce energy consumption, thereby cutting the building's CO_2 emissions. After its refurbishment, the 27-storey tower, which was built in 1981 and became the first building in Munich to exceed 100 metres in height, is to be certified as a Green Building. In order to maintain the unique visual character of the listed HVB Tower, its façade will be renovated on the inside.
The interior rooms of the high-rise will be gutted, reinterpreted as flexible and future-oriented Smart Working offices and adjusted to blend in with the exceptional design quality of its outer appearance.
The flat-roofed building structure, over which the tower floats, will receive a newly designed foyer that will do justice to its future purpose as the domicile of the management board. In its centre, a spectacularly folded space extends upwards from the ground floor over two levels.

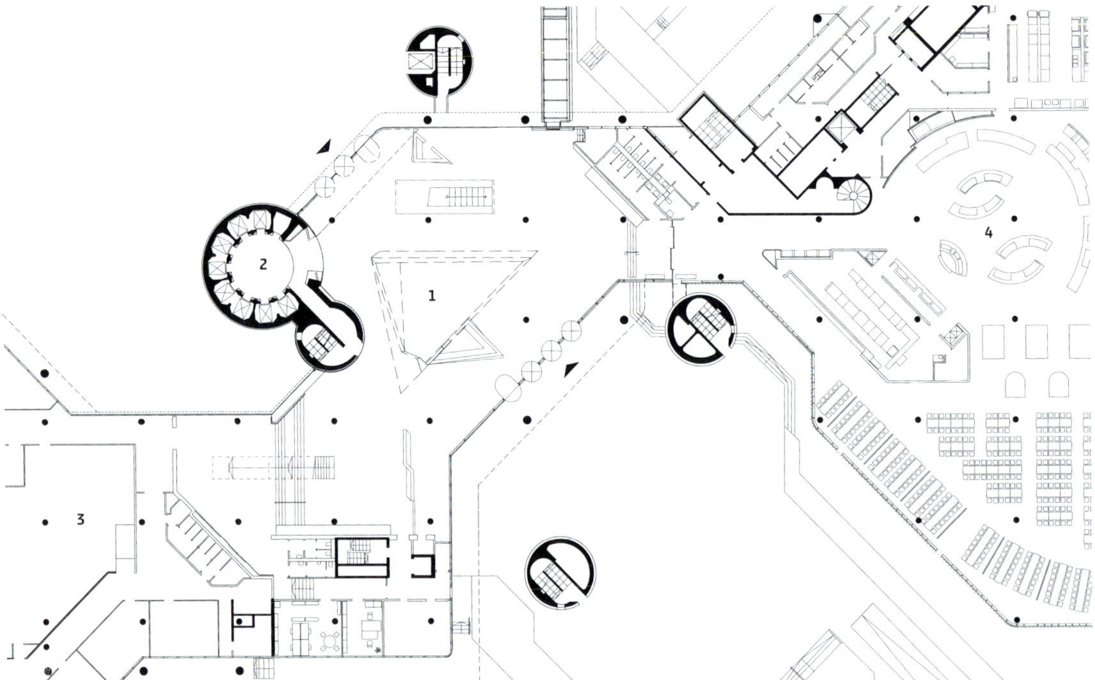
1
2
3
4

Kristalline Raumstruktur des Atriums

Crystalline spatial structure of the central atrium

1 Foyer
2 Erschließungsturm Hochhaus
3 Flachbau Nord
4 Flachbau Süd

1 Lobby
2 Circulation tower
3 Northern plinth
4 Southern plinth

schiedlichen Neigungen und Winkeln auffalten, entsteht eine vielschichtige Skulptur, die an einen geschliffenen Kristall erinnert. Die Brüstungen und die Geschosse gehen in der geometrischen Raumstruktur auf. Ein gläsernes Pultdach in Dreiecksform bildet den oberen Raumabschluss des Kristalls und lässt tagsüber Tageslicht sowie nachts Kunstlicht auf die kantigen Flächen aus mattweißem Mineralwerkstoff strömen. Die Raumskulptur stellt Sichtachsen zwischen den einzelnen Etagen her und verbindet so den Foodcourt und die Cafeteria im ersten Obergeschoss mit der multifunktionalen Veranstaltungsfläche im zweiten Stock. Sie lenkt den Blick vom Eingangsbereich des HVB-Towers nach oben. Dort zeichnet sich hinter dem Glasdach die Gestalt des 114 Meter hohen Turms ab, der die Silhouette Münchens als Wahrzeichen prägt.

Polygonal surfaces, which unfold at different inclinations and angles, create a multi-layered sculpture with a cut crystal appearance. The balustrades and floors are absorbed into the geometric spatial structure. A transparent, triangular-shaped mono-pitch roof forms the upper spatial enclosure of the crystal and allows daylight and artificial light at night to pervade the angular exteriors of the muted white solid surface. The spatial sculpture establishes axes of vision between the individual floors and in this way connects the food court and cafeteria in the first floor with the multifunctional event area on the next level. It diverts the gaze upwards, away from the entrance area of the HVB Tower, revealing behind the glass roof, the outline of the 114 metre high landmark tower which dominates the Munich skyline.

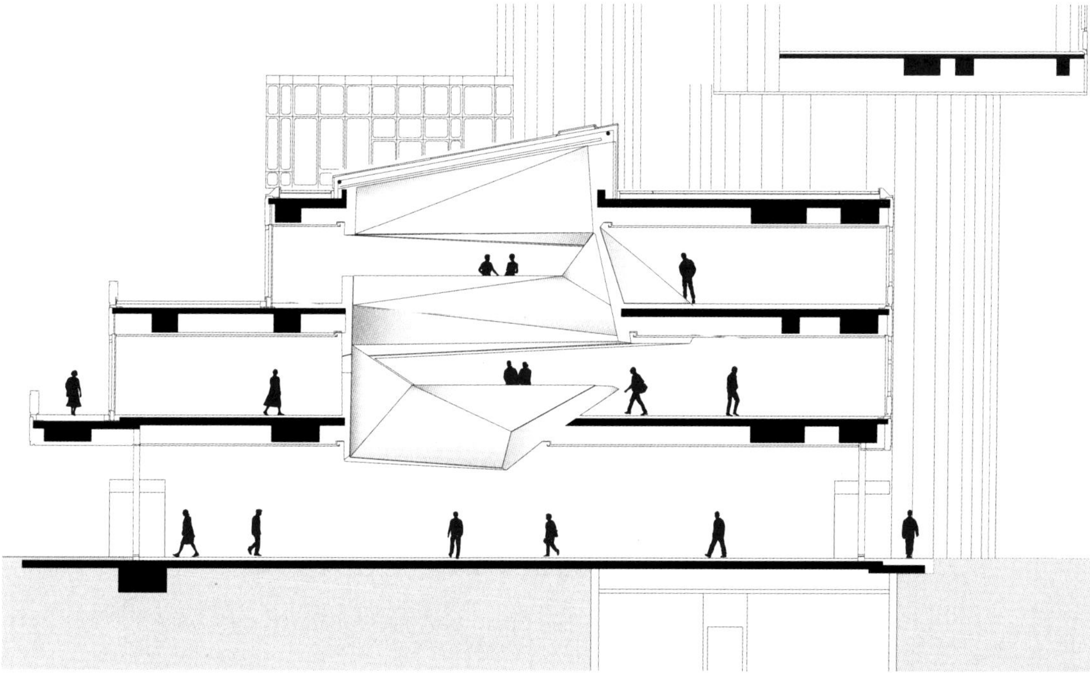

↑
Schnitt durch Eingang und Atrium im Sockelgebäude

Section through entrance and atrium in the plinth building

←
Tageslichteinfall durch das gläserne Dach des Atriums

Admission of daylight through the atrium's skylight

Modulares Innovationszentrum von Merck

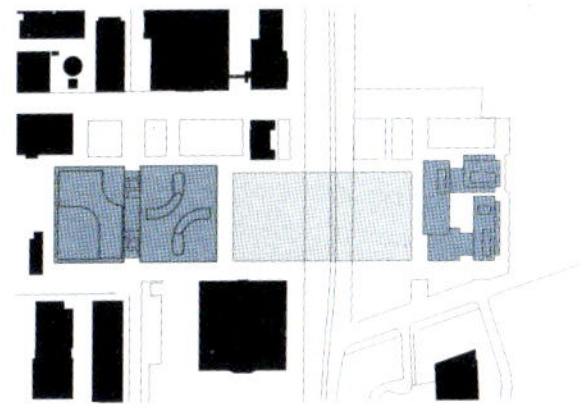

Merck KGaA
Darmstadt
2012 – 2015/2017

Tragwerksplaner
Bollinger + Grohmann, Wiesbaden
Technische Ausrüstung
ZWP, Wiesbaden
Landschaftsplaner
TOPOTEK1, Berlin
Bauphysik
Müller-BBM, Berlin
Fassadenplaner
Kucharzak, Berlin
Emmer Pfenninger Partner, CH-Münchenstein
Lichtplaner
Lumen³, München

Emanuel-Merck-Platz mit Innovationszentrum und Modularem Gebäude

Emanuel-Merck-Platz with Innovation Centre and Modular Building

Mit der strategischen Initiative ONE Global Headquarters entwickelt Merck seinen Stammsitz in Darmstadt zu einer globalen Konzernzentrale weiter. Der Masterplan für das Unternehmensgelände sieht einen neuen, zentralen Platz an der Frankfurter Straße vor, um den sich das Werksgelände von Merck, einem führenden Unternehmen für innovative und hochwertige Hightech-Produkte in den Bereichen Healthcare, Life Science und Performance Materials, gruppiert. Gerahmt von zwei Bestandsbauten, entsteht auf dem Emanuel- Merck-Platz derzeit das zukünftige Innovationszentrum. Vis-a-vis an der Ostkante des Platzes wurde ein zweigeschossiger modularer Baukörper mit einer Grundfläche von 4.000 m² errichtet, das sogenannte Modulare Innovationszentrum. Bis zur geplanten Fertigstellung des zukünftigen Innovationszentrums Ende 2017 nimmt der modulare Neubau Arbeitsflächen für wechselnde interdisziplinäre Projektteams sowie ein Gästecasino und daran angeschlossene Tagungsräume auf.

With the strategic initiative ONE Global Headquarters, Merck is continuing the development of its main site in Darmstadt into a global company headquarters. The masterplan for the company site envisages a new, central square on the Frankfurter Straße, around which the factory premises of Merck - a leading company for innovative and top-quality high-tech products in healthcare, life science and performance materials - are grouped.
Flanked by two existing buildings, the future Innovation Centre on Emanuel-Merck-Platz is currently under construction. The two-storey Modular Innovation Centre with a floor space of 4,000 m² was erected just opposite, on the eastern edge of the square. Until the future Innovation Centre is completed in 2017, the modular building's working areas will serve the needs of changing interdisciplinary research teams and includes a visitors' restaurant with connected conference rooms.

Blick aus dem Modularen Gebäude auf den Bauplatz des gegenüberliegenden Innovationszentrums am neu geschaffenen Emanuel-Merck-Platz

View from the Modular Building to the construction site of the Innovation Centre on the oppsite side of the new Emanuel-Merck-Platz

Ab 2018 soll das Gebäude dann als Besucherzentrum genutzt werden.
Der Gebäudekörper besteht aus einzelnen, gegeneinander verschobenen und teils aufeinander gestapelten Modulen, die sich um einen Innenhof gruppieren. Ein schmaler, zurückspringender Sockel hebt die einzelnen Gebäudeteile vom Boden ab und lässt sie schweben. Das Fassadenraster betont die Fugen und lässt die modulare Bauweise aus einzelnen vorgefertigten Stahlelementen erkennen. Raumhohe Fenster geben den Blick auf den großzügigen Platz und den Innenhof frei.
Am gesamten Gebäude werden mehrere, von Merck entwickelte Innovationen angewendet und getestet. Die rötlichen Lamellenelemente, die an den Südseiten des Baukörpers als Sonnenschutz dienen, enthalten farbstoffsensibilisierte Solarzellen, die Strom für einen Ein-Personen-Haushalt produzieren. In der exponierten Westfassade öffnet sich eine Fensterfront aus Liquid Crystal Windows von Merck.

From 2018 onwards the building will be used as a visitor centre.
The building consists of individual modules, grouped around an inner courtyard, some of which are staggered, some are stacked. A low, set-back plinth raises the building off the ground and creates the impression that it is floating. The façade grid emphasizes the joints and the modular construction of the individual prefabricated steel elements. Window bands extending from floor to ceiling provide views onto the spacious square and the internal courtyard. A number of Merck innovations are being put to use and tested on the building. The reddish louvres, which provide protection against the sun on the southern sides of the building, consist of dye-sensitized solar cells (DSSCs) and produce enough electrical power for a one-person household. The western façade includes a frontage with smart Liquid Crystal Windows (LCWs) designed by Merck.

←
Innenhof als offene Mitte des Modularen Gebäudes

Inner courtyard as open central space of the Modular Building

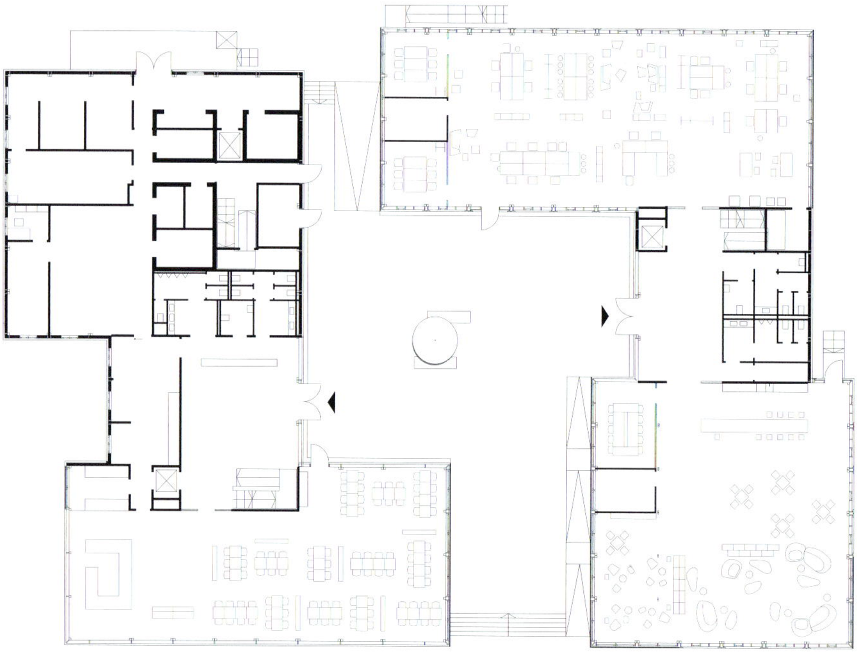

Erdgeschoss
Ground floor

↑
Fassadenelemente mit Smart Liquid Crystal Windows (LCWs) von Merck

Façade elements with Merck's Smart Liquid Crystal Windows (LCWs)

In der High-Tech-Beschichtung der Gläser wirken Flüssigkristallmoleküle wie mikroskopische Jalousien. Per Knopfdruck lassen sich die Fenster abdunkeln, sodass sie die Tagungsräume vor der Sonne schützen, ohne die Sicht auf den Platz zu beeinträchtigen. Die Verwendung von Technologien wie den farbstoffsensibilisierten, organischen Solarzellen und den intelligenten Flüssigkristallfenstern macht das Modulgebäude zu einem Vorzeigeprojekt für Innovationen von Morgen.

The molecules in the high-tech coating of the windows act as microscopic venetian blinds. The windows can be darkened at the press of a button to protect the conference rooms from daylight, without any adverse effects on the view out to the square. The use of technologies such as dye-sensitized solar cells and smart Liquid Crystal Windows make the modular building a pioneering project for the innovations of tomorrow.

↖
Module mit Arbeitsflächen für wechselnde interdisziplinäre Forschungsteams

Modules with workspaces for changing interdisciplinary research teams

Bewegliche Sonnenschutzlamellen mit farbstoffsensibilisierten Solarzellen (DSSCs) von Merck

Movable sun protection lamellae with dye-sensitized solar cells (DSSCs) by Merck

Bürohaus Europacity

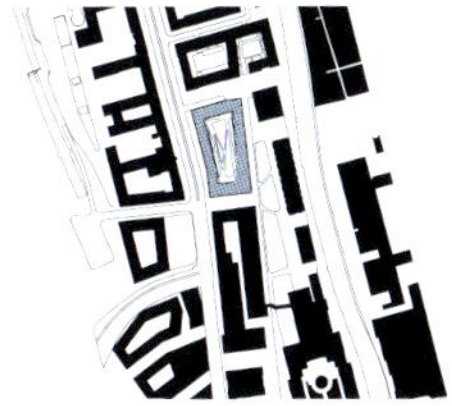

CA Immo
Berlin
2015 - 2018

Bürogebäude in unmittelbarer Umgebung zum Berliner Hauptbahnhof

New office building in close vicinity to Berlin Main Station

Die Machbarkeitsstudie für das Bürohaus an der Heidestraße in Berlin-Mitte sieht zwei Bauphasen für den westlichen sowie den östlichen Gebäudetrakt vor. Gemeinsam bilden die beiden U-förmigen Flügel einen durchgängigen fünfgeschossigen Block mit zentralem Innenhof.

Die Kubatur des 117 Meter langen Gebäudes greift den Knick der Heidestraße auf und macht ihn zur Grundlage seines Gestaltungskonzepts. Die Fassade ist in drei doppelgeschossige, gegeneinander versetzte Bänder gegliedert, die sich überschneiden und mal vor-, dann wieder zurückspringen. Ihre differenzierte Ausrichtung ergibt sich aus den versetzten nördlichen und südlichen Straßenfluchten sowie aus dem tatsächlichen Straßenverlauf. Die Metallpaneele und Glasflächen der einzelnen Fassadenbänder variieren in der Breite und sind zu einem spannungsreichen Rhythmus gefügt. So entsteht ein Spiel aus Offenheit und Geschlossenheit, das die Dynamik des gestapelten Volumens stärkt. Der Haupteingang und das Foyer liegen unter der Auskragung im Süden.

The feasibility study for the office building on Heidestrasse envisages two construction phases for the western and the eastern wing. Combined, the two U-shaped wings form a continuous five-storey block with a central internal courtyard.

The shape of the 117 metre long building follows the kink in Heidestrasse, thus making it a principle of the building's design concept. The façade is divided into three double-storey bands continually projecting or recessing to varying degrees in or out with respect to one another. Their changing individual orientations arise from the offset northern and southern road alignments and the actual road layout. The metal panels and glass areas of the façade bands vary in width and join together to create an exciting rhythm in an interplay of openness and solidity that strengthens the dynamic of the stacked volume.

The main entrance and the foyer stand under the cantilever in the south. The individual storeys are connected to one another by five stairways and lift cores.

1
1
2
2
2
2
2

1
1
1
1
1
3
3
3
3
3
3
2
Heidestraße

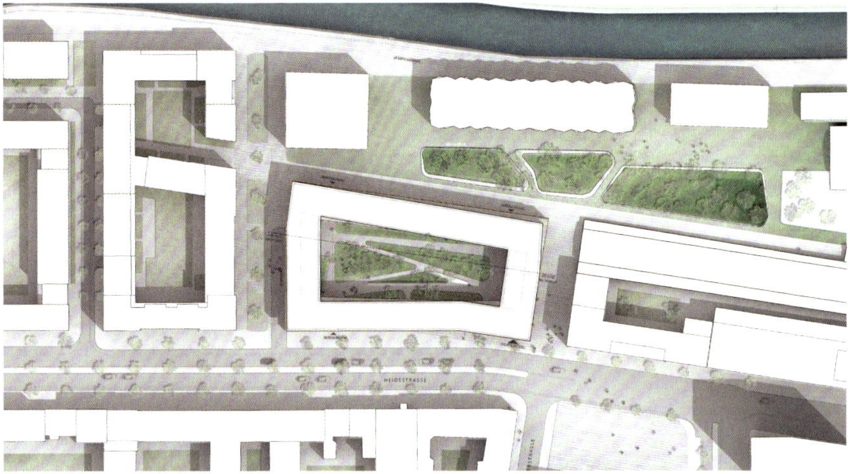

←
Obergeschoss
1 Großraumbüro
2 Kombibüro

Upper level
1 Open plan office
2 Combi office

Die einzelnen Geschosse sind durch fünf Treppen- und Aufzugskerne miteinander verbunden. Die Büroflächen von insgesamt 28.500 m² sind in Nutzungseinheiten von jeweils maximal 600 m² eingeteilt. Das Fassadenraster von 1,35 Metern ist auf die Organisation der Innenräume übertragen. So können nach Bedarf flexible Trennwände auch für die Arbeitsplätze entlang der Fassade eingezogen werden.

The total office space of 28,500 m² is divided into usage units no larger than 600 m² in area. The 1.35 metre façade grid is transferred onto the organisation of the interior spaces. If necessary, the flexible partition walls can also be installed for the work stations along the façade.

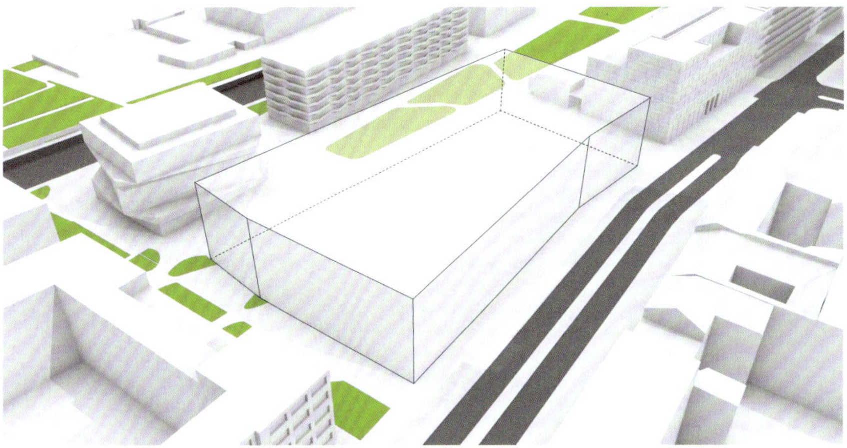

←
Erdgeschoss
1 Foyer
2 Meetingraum
3 Büro

Ground level
1 Foyer
2 Meeting rooms
3 Office

TAXI

BMW FIZ Future Hybridgebäude

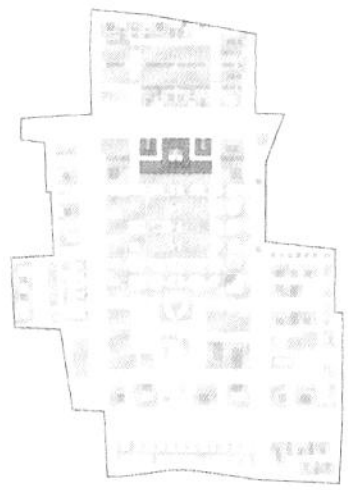

BMW Group
München
2014 – 2019/2020

Technische Ausrüstung
Climaplan, München
Tragwerksplaner
SSF Ingenieure, München
Bauphysik
PMI, Unterhaching
Landschaftsplaner
TOPOTEK 1, Berlin
Infrastruktur
Regierungsbaumeister Schlegel, München
Brandschutz
Kersken + Kirchner, München
Küchenplaner
IGW Ingenieurgruppe Walter, Stuttgart
Aufzugsplanung
iFH Ingenieurbüro Felka-Hoffmann, Weihenzell

Gemäß den Vorgaben des FIZ Future Masterplans wird das Forschungs- und Innovationszentrum (FIZ) der BMW Group in München schrittweise erweitert. Der Entwurf für den 1. Bauabschnitt im Norden des Geländes sieht einen Gebäudekomplex vor, der ein Pendant zum bestehenden Projekthaus Süd bildet und über eine zentrale Achse mit ihm verbunden ist. Die hybriden Gebäudestrukturen der Neubauten vernetzen einzelne, funktional getrennte Bereiche miteinander. Insgesamt sollen die neuen Flächen für Werkstatt, Prüfstand und Montage sowie für Büros und Servicefunktionen ein neues Arbeitsumfeld für 3.200 Mitarbeiter schaffen und 2019 bezogen werden.
In das Projekthaus Nord führt die Magistrale, die als zentrale Organisationsachse des Masterplankonzeptes zukünftig die Werkstätten und Fachbereiche von Süden nach Norden erschließen wird. Die Magistrale ist pulsierendes Zentrum des FIZ, sie stärkt den interdisziplinären Austausch zwischen einzelnen Bereichen, die sich entlang der Achse aufreihen und durch sie verbunden sind.

The BMW Group's Research and Innovation Centre (FIZ) in Munich is being extended in stages according to the recommendations of the FIZ Future masterplan. The design for the 1st Building Phase in the north of the site makes provision for a building complex that forms a counterpart to the existing Project House South and is connected to it by means of a central axis. The hybrid building structures of the new buildings link the different functional areas with one another.
Altogether, the new areas for the workshop, test bench and assembly, offices and service functions will establish an innovative working environment for 3,200 employees and are scheduled to be occupied by 2019.
The Project House North is connected to the central axis, which, as the main communication spine of the masterplan concept, will establish a north-south link to the workshops and specialist areas. This spine will be the pulsating heart of the Research and Innovation Centre; it sustains interdisciplinary communication between the individual sectors along its length.

Magistrale als zentrale Kommunikationsachse

The central axis as main communication spine

Verbindungachse vom geplanten Eingang Süd zum FIZ Nord

Connections along the spine from the future southern entrance to FIZ North

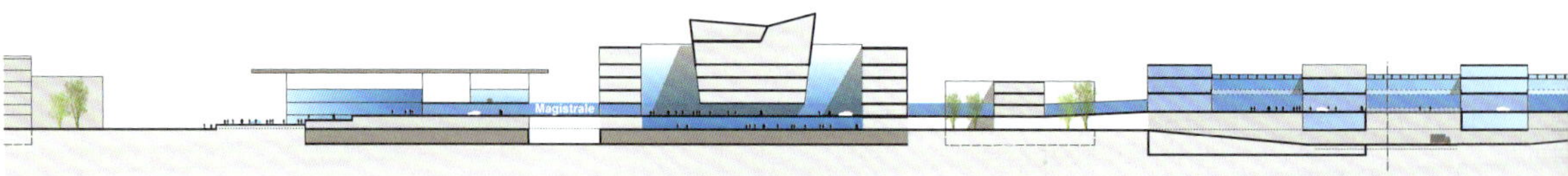

Eingang Süd FIZ Forum
Southern entrance FIZ Forum

Projekthaus
Project House

Büromodul
Office module

Werkstattbereiche
Workshop areas

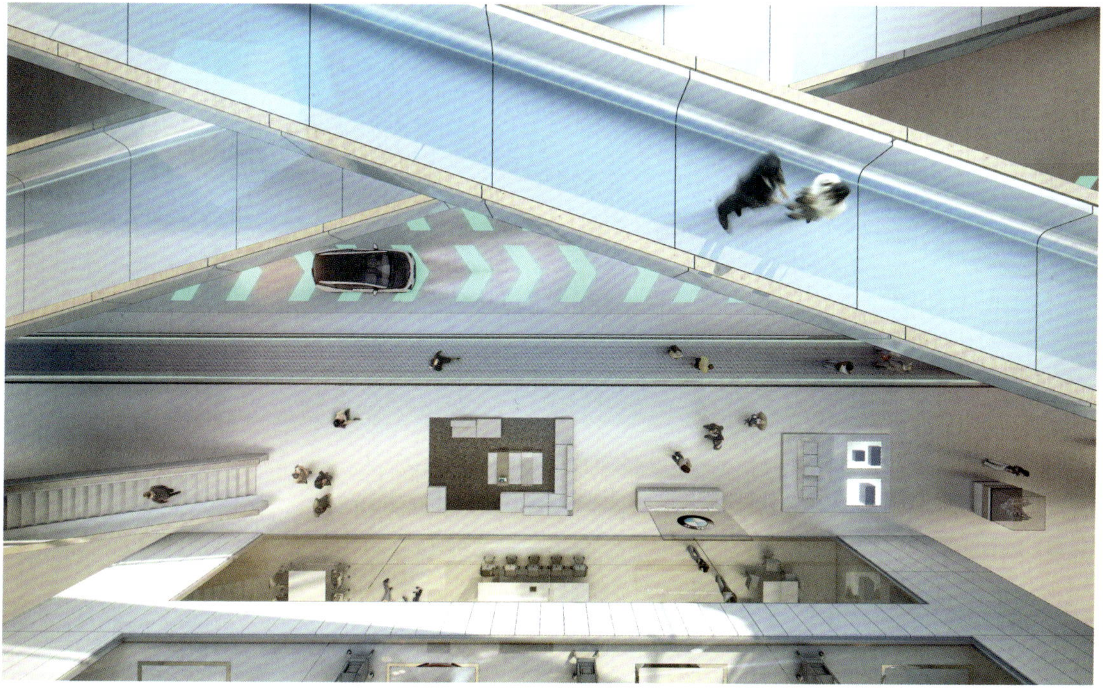

Wissensaustausch von Experten entlang der Magistrale

Exchange of expert knowledge along the communication spine

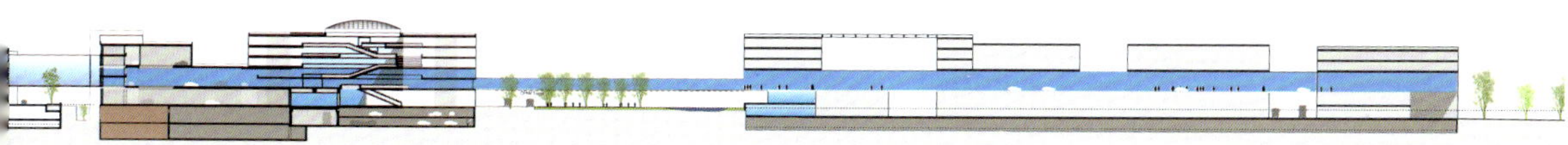

WPM-Gebäude
WPM Building

Projekthaus Nord
Project House North

Erweiterung Nord Nord
Extension north north

Eingang Nord
Northern entrance

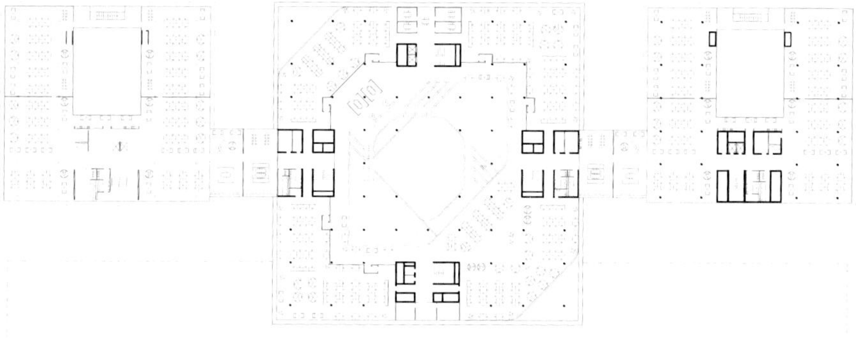

↗
4. Obergeschoss Projekthaus mit Büromodulen

Project House, fourth floor, with office modules

←
Zentrale Kommunikationshalle
Central communication hall

Die zentrale Halle bildet einen offenen Kommunikationsraum, der Wege bündelt und einzelne Geschosse sowie ihre Büroflächen visuell miteinander verbindet. Auf den Balkons in den oberen Stockwerken des Atriums befinden sich flexible Arbeitszonen, die die Büroflächen entlang der verglasten Fassaden ergänzen und Raum für die Vernetzung der Arbeitsprozesse schaffen. Das durchgängige Sockelgeschoss verbindet das Projekthaus mit flankierenden weiteren Büromodulen und wird eine Kantine mit 1.200 Sitzplätzen aufnehmen. Ein ebenerdiger Boulevard und die Logistikstraße erschließen den Neubau in Ost-West-Richtung innerhalb des FIZ-Geländes.
Im südlichen Teil des Baufelds entsteht ein Gebäude mit Werkstatt-, Prüfstands- und Montagebereichen (WPM) sowie werkstattnahen Büros in den Zwischenebenen. Der 220 Meter lange Gebäuderiegel überbaut die bestehende Crashanlage, seine Flächen gehen nahtlos in das Projekthaus Nord über. Durch diese Überlagerungen entstehen Vernetzungsbereiche, in denen die Mitarbeiter der Entwicklungsbereiche und Werkstätten zusammenarbeiten können.

The central hall forms an open communication space, which brings together communication routes and visually connects the individual floors and offices with one another. Flexible working zones on the balconies in the upper storeys of the atrium enhance the office areas along the glazed façades and create space to interlink the various work processes. The continuous plinth storey, which connects the Project House with adjacent office modules, will also accommodate a canteen capable of 1,200 seats.
A ground-level boulevard and the logistics road connect the new building along the east-west axis within the FIZ campus.
For the southern part of the site, a building with workshop, test benches and assembly areas is planned, with supporting offices on the mezzanine floors. The 220 metre long building block, which is built above the existing crash bed facility, transitions smoothly into the Project House North. This creates interaction areas for both development engineers and workshop teams.

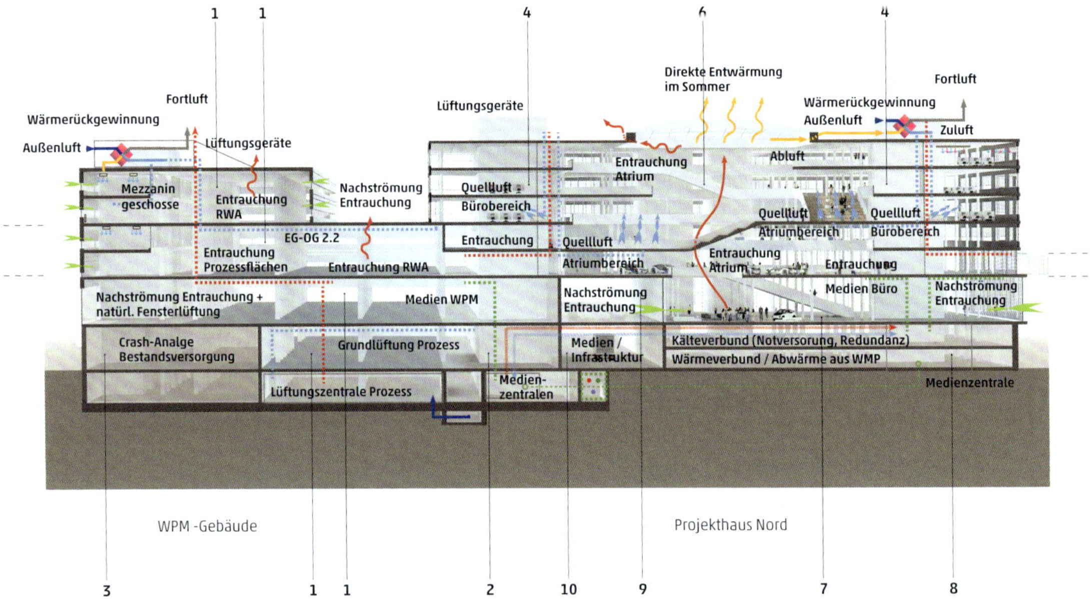

1 **Labore, Prüfstände, Werkstätten**
2 **Logistik**
3 **Crashanlage**
4 **Bürobereiche Projekthaus Nord**
5 **Sondernutzung Atrium, zukünftige Magistrale**
6 **Zentrales Atrium**
7 **Eingangsbereich**
8 **Parken**
9 **Boulevard**
10 **Logistikstraße**

1 Laboratory, Test benches, Workshops
2 Logistics
3 Crash Test Facility
4 Offices Project Building North
5 Special Use Atrium, Future Communication Spine
6 Central Atrium
7 Main Entrance
8 Parking Area
9 Boulevard
10 Logistics Streets

Schnitt durch das Hybridgebäude mit Projekthaus Nord und WPM-Gebäude

Section through the Hybrid Building with Northern Project Building and WPM Building

→
Grundriss 1. Obergeschoss
Floor plan first floor

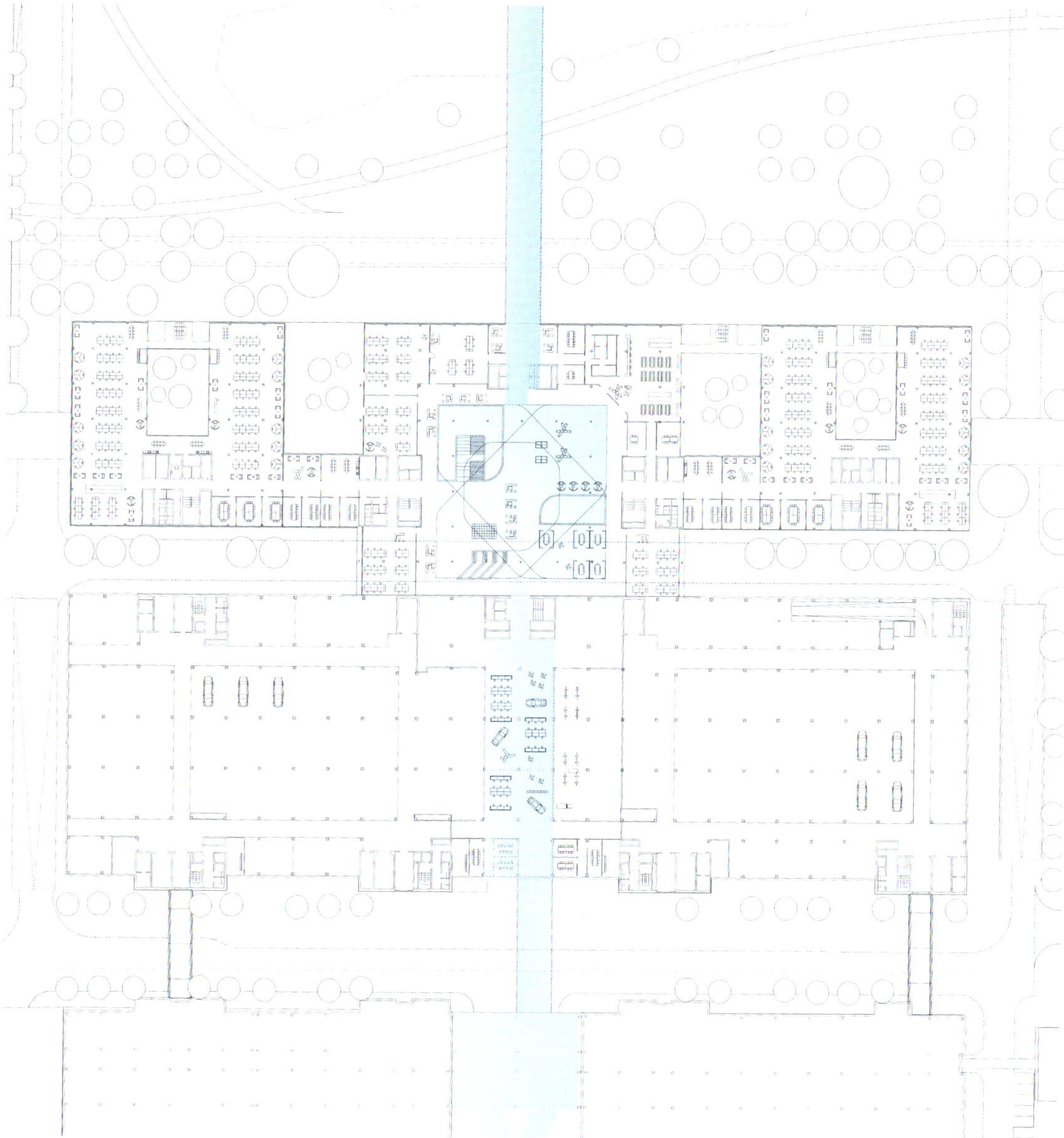

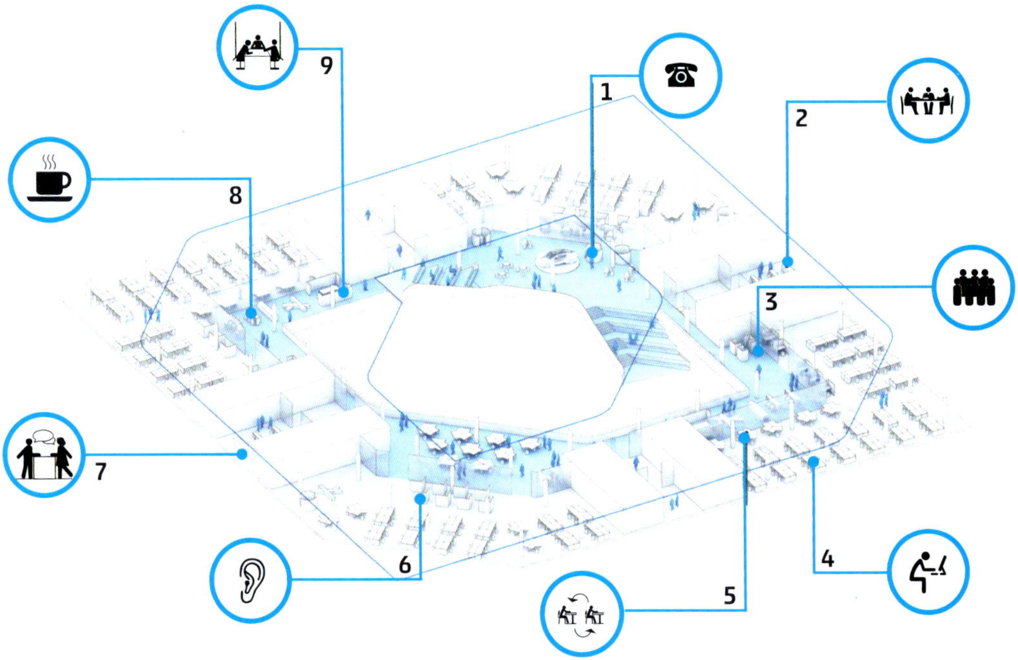

Neue Arbeitswelten

1 **Phone Booth**
2 **Besprechung**
3 **Team Bench**
4 **Home-base**
5 **Co-Working**
6 **Focus-Area**
7 **Stand-Up-Meeting**
8 **Informal Meeting**
9 **Think Tank**

New Working Environments

1 Phone Booth
2 Conference
3 Team Bench
4 Home-base
5 Co-Working
6 Focus-Area
7 Stand-Up-Meeting
8 Informal Meeting
9 Think Tank

→
Teamflächen (oben) und offene Kommunikationszonen um das Atrium

Team areas (top) and open communication zones around the atrium

Haikou International Financial Centre plot A und B

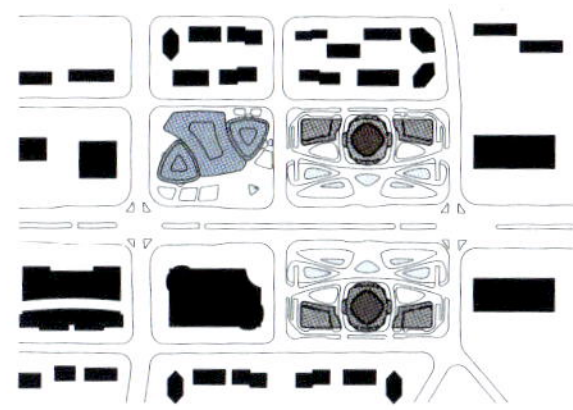

Hainan Airlines
Haikou, China
2013 – 2022

Technische Ausrüstung
IPPR International Engineering Corporation, Beijing
Review Engineer
Parsons Brinckerhoff, New York
Tragwerksplaner
Arup, London
Review Engineer
Thornton Tomasetti, New York
Fassadenplaner
Front, New York
KWP Konstruct West Partners, Hongkong

Lokaler Planungspartner
IPPR International Engineering Corporation, Beijing

Im neuen Geschäftsviertel der südchinesischen Millionenmetropole Haikou werden drei Gebäude im Rahmen des Masterplans realisiert. Die beiden 430 Meter hohen Türme auf plot A im Zentrum des Areals haben städtebauliche Signalwirkung und werden zu Landmarks für das gesamte Quartier. Das erste Hochhaus ist bereits im Bau, das zweite auf der gegenüberliegenden Straßenseite wird sich in seiner Struktur und Außenwirkung an ihm orientieren. Die beiden Türme zeichnen sich durch eine hochperformative, intelligente Gebäudehülle aus, die auf das tropische Klima der Insel Hainan reagiert. In ihrer unmittelbaren Nachbarschaft entsteht das Haikou International Financial Centre plot B mit einer Einkaufspassage und zwei weitere bis zu 47 Stockwerke hohen Bürotürmen. Der Gebäudekomplex soll aufgrund seiner Lage zwischen dem Stadtzentrum und dem neuen Geschäftsbezirk vermitteln. Er leitet von den kantigen Bestandsbauten der Umgebung zur komplexen Kubatur der beiden zentralen Hochhäuser über und schafft durch seine beiden 220 und 174 Meter hohen Bürogebäude einen formalen Übergang.

Three buildings are to be built according to the masterplan in the new business quarter of Haikou, a city of a million people in southern China. The two 430 metre high towers in plot A in the centre of the area will have a significant effect on urban development and will become landmarks for the whole district. The first high-rise is already under construction, the second on the opposite side of the road will be similar in layout and external appearance. The twin towers are characterised by a highly performative intelligent building envelope which responds to the tropical climate on the island of Hainan.
The Haikou International Financial Centre plot B with a shopping arcade and two office towers, will take shape with up to 47-storeys. Because of its location, the building complex mediates between the city centre and the new business area. It conducts the eye from the rectangular existing buildings to the organic shape of the two high-rises and, through its 220 and 174 metre-high office buildings, creates a flowing transition.

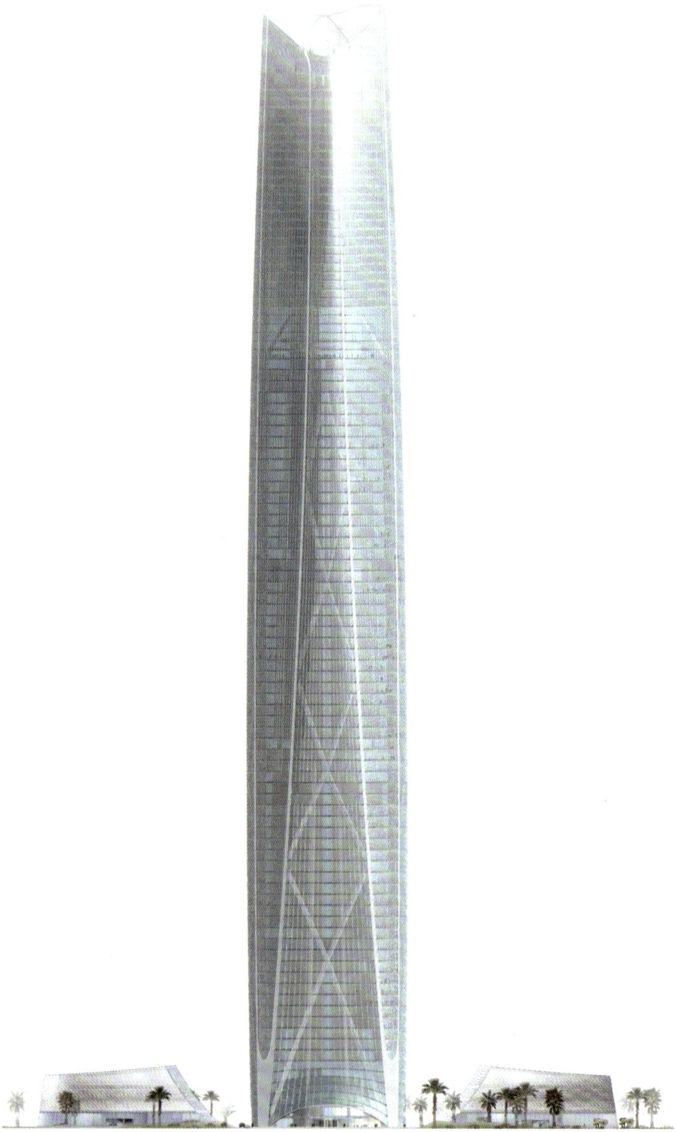

Primärstruktur
Primary structure

+

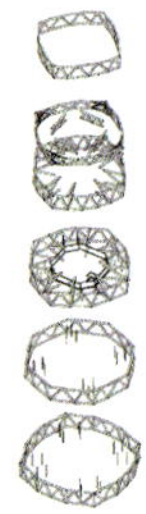

Sekundärstruktur
Secondary structure

+

Strukturen kombiniert
Structures combined

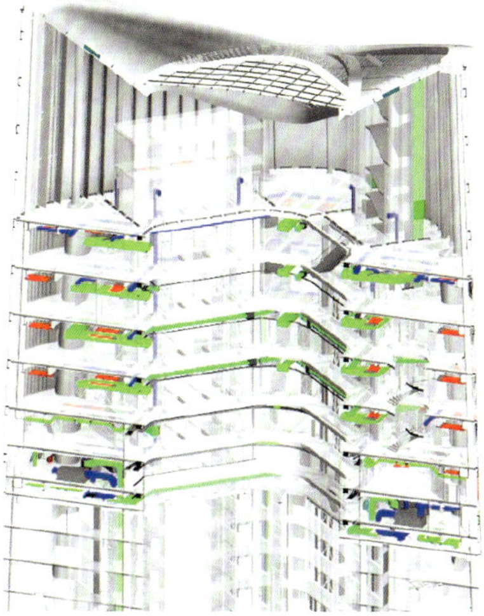

Haikou Tower, BIM-Modell Turmspitze
Haikou Tower, BIM model tower tip

BIM-Modell Podium
BIM model podium

Erdbeben-Simulation
Earthquake shaking table

Fundament-Belastungstest
Foundation load test

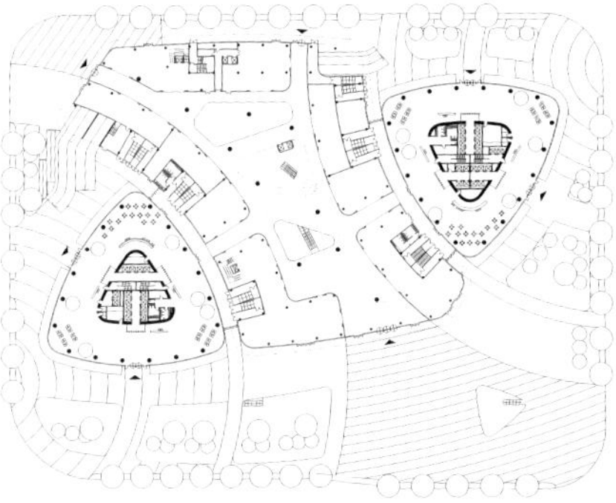

Die beiden Türme sind durch einen frei geformten Zwischenbau mit fünf Geschossen für Geschäfte und Restaurants miteinander verbunden. Die öffentlichen Passagen in dem Gebäude lenken die Fußgänger ins Stadtzentrum und führen sie gleichzeitig zu den beiden diagonal platzierten Bürotürmen. Nach außen präsentiert sich der Zwischenbau mit einer kleinteiligen Fassade, die medial bespielt wird. Die beiden Bürotürme hingegen greifen die vertikale Dynamik der zentralen Landmark-Hochhäuser des Geschäftsbezirks auf. Ihre Außenhaut besteht je nach Himmelsrichtung und Höhe aus unterschiedlich geschlossenen und transparenten Fassadenelementen. Im Wechsel der beiden Gestaltungsmuster entsteht ein wirkungsvolles Flirren, das den optischen Gesamteindruck des International Financial Centre ausmacht.

The two towers are connected by a free-form intermediate building with five storeys for shops and restaurants. The public passages in the building direct the pedestrians simultaneously towards the city centre and the two diagonally opposed office towers.
The outside of the intermediate building presents itself as a fragmented media-oriented façade. The two office high-rises on the other hand take up the vertical dynamic of the central landmark of the business district. Their external skins consist of solid and transparent façade elements depending on the direction and height. Their changing surface patterns create an impressive shimmer which characterizes the overall visual impression of the International Financial Centre.

International Financial Centre plot B mit einer Einkaufspassage und zwei bis zu 47 Stockwerke hohen Bürotürmen

International Financial Centre plot B with shopping mall and two office towers up to 47-storeys

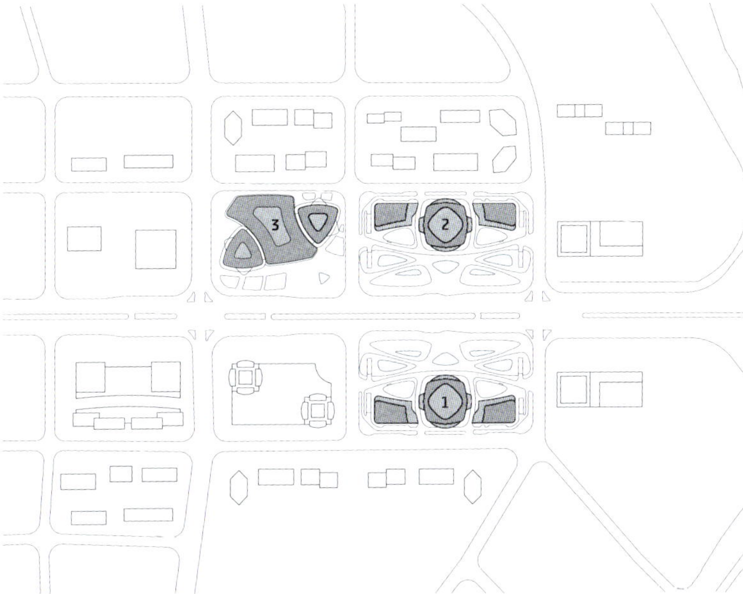

1 Haikou Tower im Bau Fertigstellung 2022
2 International Financial Centre plot A in Planung
3 International Financial Centre plot B in Planung

1 Haikou Tower under construction Completion 2022
2 International Financial Centre plot A Design stage
3 International Financial Centre plot B Design stage

Das plot B leitet von den kantigen Bestandsbauten der Umgebung zur komplexen Kubatur der beiden zentralen Hochhäuser über

Plot B leads the eye from the rectangular existing buildings to the organic shape of the Haikou Towers and creates a flowing transition

China Railway Tower

China Railway Engineering Group
Taiyuan, China
2013 – 2017

Lokaler Planungspartner
Taiyuan Architectural Design Institute

Wettbewerb 2013
1. Preis

Competition 2013
1st Prize

Der 174 Meter hohe Turm der China Railway Engineering in Taiyuan steht auf einem Eckgrundstück nahe des Zentrums der zentralchinesischen Millionenmetropole. In ihm befinden sich insgesamt 60.000 m² Bürofläche, die teils vom Bauherren genutzt und teils vermietet werden sollen. Das Hochhaus greift durch seinen orthogonalen Abschluss den Ost-West-Verlauf der Straßenachsen auf. Der oktogonale Grundriss im Erdgeschoss hingegen schafft vielseitige Bezugspunkte zur Umgebung. Die Erschließung des Turms mit Haupteingängen in allen Himmelsrichtungen unterstreicht seinen offenen Charakter.
Die Glasfassade des Hochhauses ist durch ein einheitliches Gestaltungsprinzip rhythmisiert. Schmale Lisenen gliedern die Fassadenflächen und strecken sich als durchgängige Bänder bis zur Turmspitze. Die Metallelemente strukturieren die Teilfassaden in einer vertikalen Gegenbewegung aus sich verjüngenden und breiter werdenden Intervallen. Ihr wechselnder Rhythmus sorgt für ein spannungsreiches Erscheinungsbild, das die Kubatur des Hochhauses betont.

The 174 metre high China Railway Engineering Tower in Taiyuan stands on a corner site close to the centre of the central Chinese million-strong metropolis. The building contains 60,000 m² of office space, part of which is to be used by the client and part leased to others. The orthogonal termination of this high-rise conforms with the east-west orientation of the road grid. The octagonal shape in plan of the ground floor on the other hand creates many-sided reference points for the surrounding area. The circulation plan for the tower with main entrances at all cardinal points of the compass emphasises the building's open character.
A consistent design principle imposes a rhythm on the tower's glass façade. Narrow lesenes divide the façade surface and stretch as continuous strips right up to the top of the tower. The metal elements structure the façade sections in a vertical counter movement of tapering and widening intervals. Their changing rhythm creates an exciting appearance that emphasises the shape of the high-rise.

中铁三局

1 Ausgangsvolumen
Generic mass

2 Zugangssituationen Vorplatz
Entrance scenarios from forecourt

3 Verfeinerung und Flächenkrümmung
Refinement and curvature

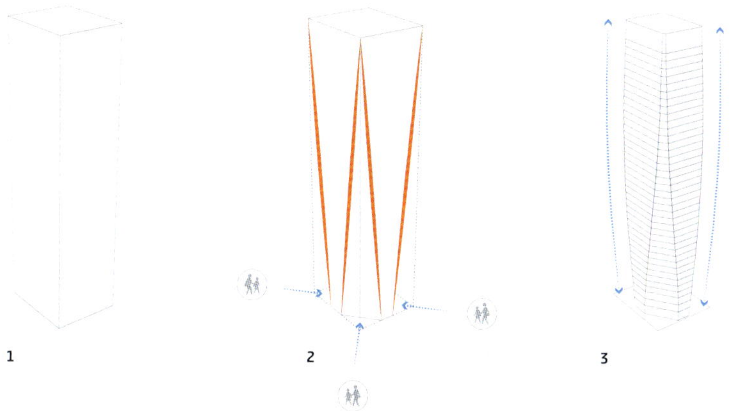

Der zentrale Erschließungskern in der Mitte des Turms bündelt die Aufzüge, mit denen Besucher bis zur Sky-Lounge in den beiden letzten Geschossen gelangen. Mit durchgängigen Fensterfronten, die sich teils auch im Dach fortsetzen, ist der Bereich maximal transparent gestaltet. So können die Gäste der Bar und des Restaurants uneingeschränkt auf die Skyline der Stadt blicken.

The main circulation core in the middle of the tower groups together the lifts that carry the visitors to the sky lounge on the top two floors. With continuous windowed frontages which extend in some places into the roof, this area is designed to provide maximum transparency. The guests can enjoy unobstructed views of the city skyline from the bar and restaurant.

←
China Railway Tower im Rohbau 2015

China Railway Tower structural work 2015

↓
Nächste Seite links: Eingangsgeschoss mit Aufzugslobby und Wartelounge rechts: Skybar mit Restaurant

Following page left: Entrance level with elevator lobby and waiting lounge right: Skybar with restaurant

CHANGAN
CHANGAN

Chang'an R&D Centre

Chang'an Automobile Co. Ltd.
Chongqing, China
2012 – 2017

Lokaler Planungspartner
Chongqing Tongcheng Engineering Consulting Design

Zentraler Eingang
Central entrance

Das Research and Development Centre steht im Mittelpunkt des neuen Unternehmensstandorts des Automobilherstellers Chang'an. Der Neubau liegt in zentraler Position auf einer Landschaftsachse, die das weitläufige Werksgelände im zentralchinesischen Yuzi von Osten nach Westen durchquert. Durch den großen vorgelagerten Platz hebt sich der Baukörper von den umliegenden Produktionshallen ab und wird zum Landmark für das gesamte Unternehmensareal. Die Gebäudeform greift eine traditionelle chinesische Typologie mit einer Sockelzone und einem überhängenden Dach auf. Zwei horizontale, geschossübergreifende Schichten gliedern die Fassade und kragen in den oberen Etagen 9 Meter aus. Die Flächen in dem fünfgeschossigen Gebäude mit quadratischem Grundriss sind um einen zentralen Innenhof verteilt. Die einzelnen Forschungseinrichtungen und Büros sind durch eine Erschließungszone mit einem Café, einer Bibliothek und Ausstellungsräumen verbunden. Die Diagonale durch den Innenhof führt die Landschaftsachse durch das Gebäude und verlängert sie bis zum höher gelegenen Design Centre.

The Research and Development Centre lies at the heart of the new corporate site of the carmaker Chang'an. The new building is located at a central position on a landscape axis, which crosses the extensive factory premises from east to west in the central Chinese district of Yuzi. Due to its location and prominent frontal position, the Research and Development Centre stands out from the surrounding production buildings and becomes a landmark for the entire company premises. The building's shape follows a traditional Chinese typology, with a plinth area and overhanging roof. The façade is divided into two horizontal layers which span the floors. The upper floors project out like a pulpit over a length of 9 metres. The floor areas in the five-storey building with quadratic floor plan are distributed around a central inner courtyard. The individual research facilities and offices are connected by a multi-functional central access zone with a café, exhibition room and library. A diagonal corridor crosses the square inner courtyard, leading the landscape axis through the building and up to the higher-level Design Centre.

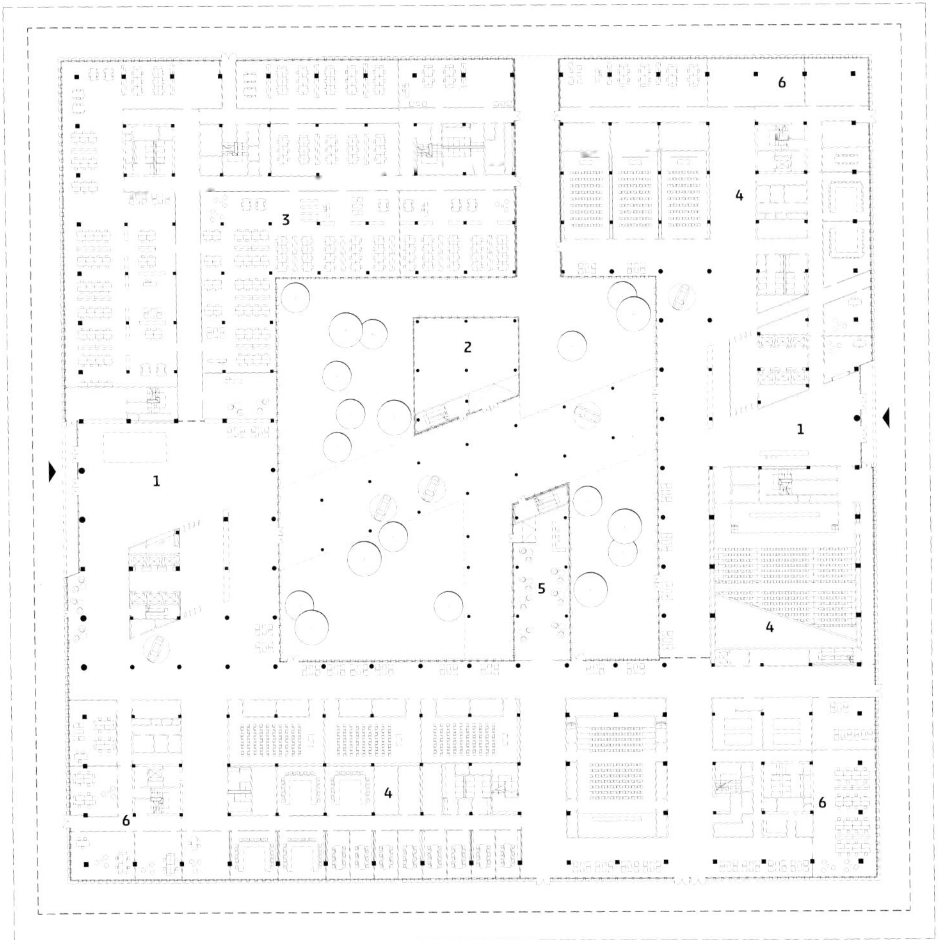

Grundriss
1 Lobby
2 Ausstellung
3 Büro
4 Besprechung/Konferenz
5 Café
6 Support

Ground floor
1 Lobby
2 Exhibition
3 Office
4 Meeting/Conference
5 Café
6 Support

Freier Innenhof im Erdgeschoss

Open court yard on the ground floor

Eingangslobby

Main entrance lobby

← ↑
Eingang Entwicklungsgelände Allee durch die Produktionsbauten

The entrance to the development area is reached via a tree-lined boulevard through production

↗
Design Centre auf dem Hochplateau mit Blick auf das tiefer gelegene R&D Centre und die Produktion

Design Centre with a view from the higher levels of the site on to the lower-lying R&D Centre and production buildings

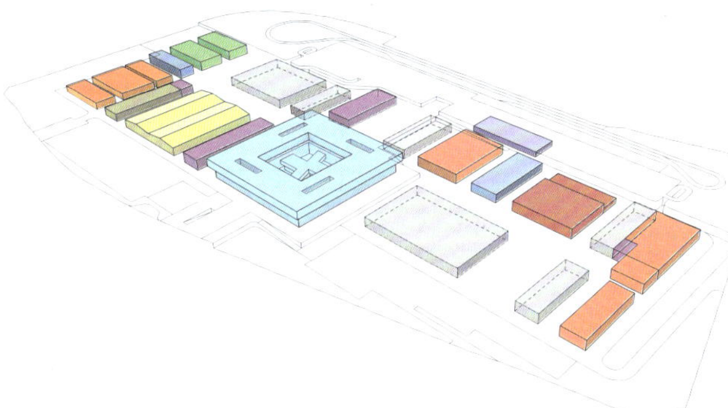

Testlabore	Test Laboratories
Testgebäude	Test Building
Motorenzentrum	Engine Centre
Lagergebäude	Storage
Fahrzeugproduktion	Vehicle Production
Betriebsgastronomie	Company Restaurant
Hauptgebäude	Main Building
Energiezentrale	Power Station
GDC	GDC
Erweiterung	Expansion

Bendix Corporate Headquarters

Bendix
Cleveland, Ohio
2015 – 2017

Lokaler Planungspartner
Westlake Reed Leskosky, Cleveland

Der Masterplan für das Bendix Corporate Headquarters setzt die Ergebnisse eines vorausgehenden Programming-Verfahrens um. Die Konzeptstudie strukturiert das 50.500 m^2 große Unternehmensareal mit den zukünftigen Headquarters des US-amerikanischen Tochterkonzerns von Knorr-Bremse in Cleveland, Ohio, und sieht ein zentrales Forschungs- und Entwicklungszentrum vor.

In dem Gebäude entsteht ein vernetztes, interdisziplinäres Arbeitsumfeld für 700 Mitarbeiter, das den Wissensaustausch fördert. Die Labore und Prüfstände des Herstellers für Bremssysteme von Lastkraftwagen nehmen insgesamt 10.000 m^2 Fläche ein. Sie sind durch kurze Wege und Kommunikationszonen mit den Büroflächen der unterschiedlichen Departments und Kompetenzzentren auf insgesamt 15.000 m^2 verbunden. Mit der Option eines rückwärtigen Anbaus sollen die Flächen bei Bedarf ergänzt werden können.

The masterplan for the Bendix Corporate Headquarters implements the results of a preliminary programming process. The concept study structures the 50,500 m^2 company site containing the future headquarters of the US-American subsidiary of Knorr-Bremse in Cleveland, Ohio and envisages a pivotal research and development centre.

An integrated, interdisciplinary working environment is to be created for 700 employees in the building, in which the exchange of knowledge will be promoted. A total of 10,000 m^2 of space will be provided for laboratory and test benches of the truck brake system manufacturer. These will be connected by short distances and communication zones to the various departments and competence centres which will cover an area of 15,000 m^2. The floor area can be extended if required with an option of a set-back extension.

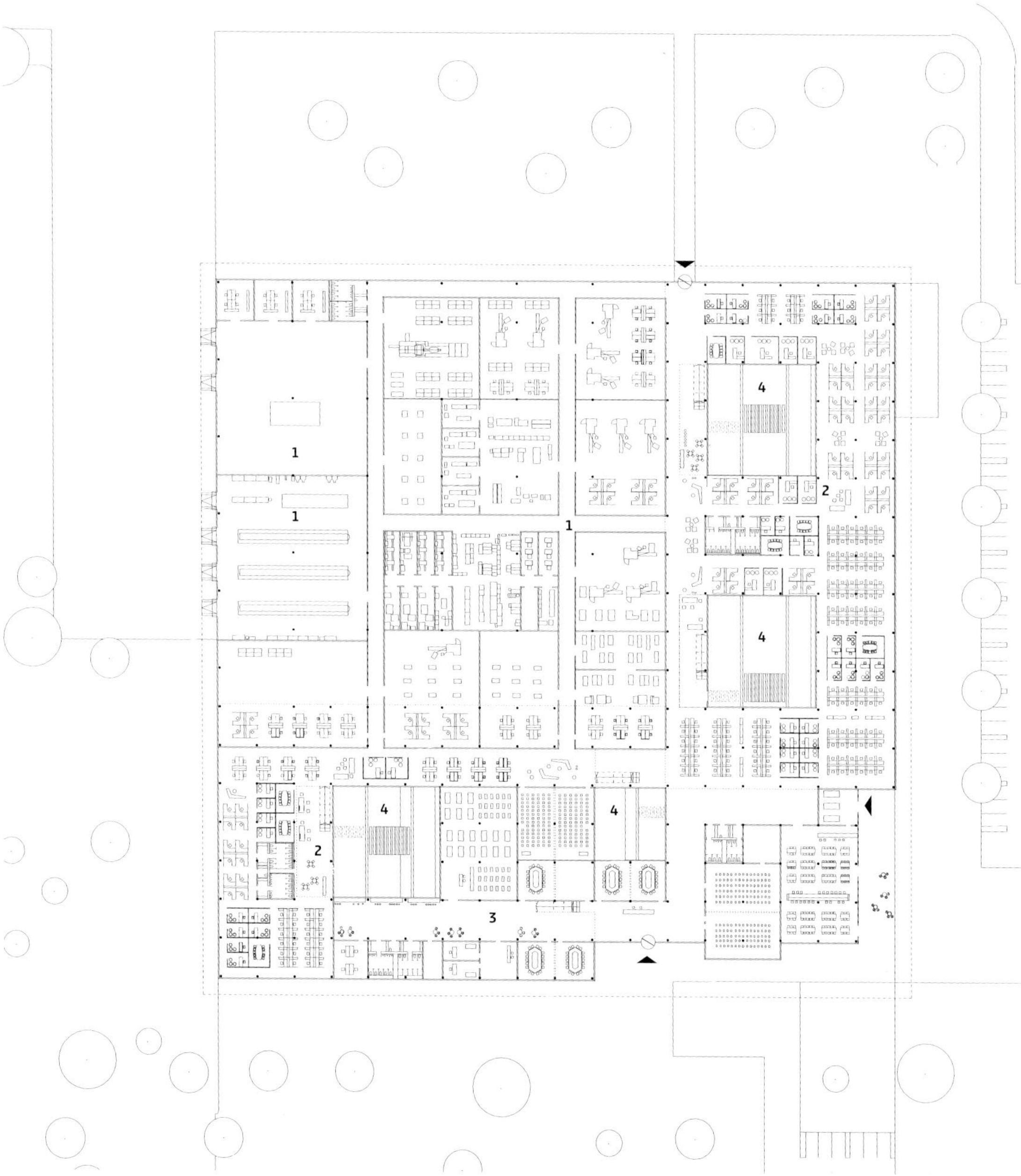
1
1
1
4
2
4
4
2
4
3

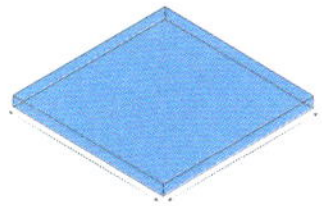

Grundform
Base Geometry

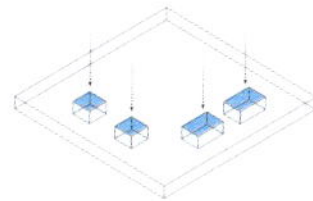

Innenhöfe
Courtyards

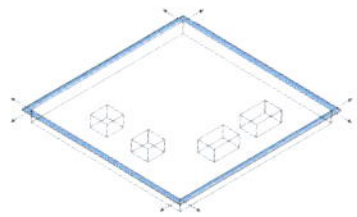

Dachvorsprünge
Roof Eaves

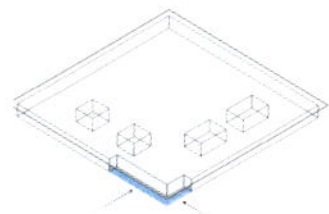

Eingang
Entrance

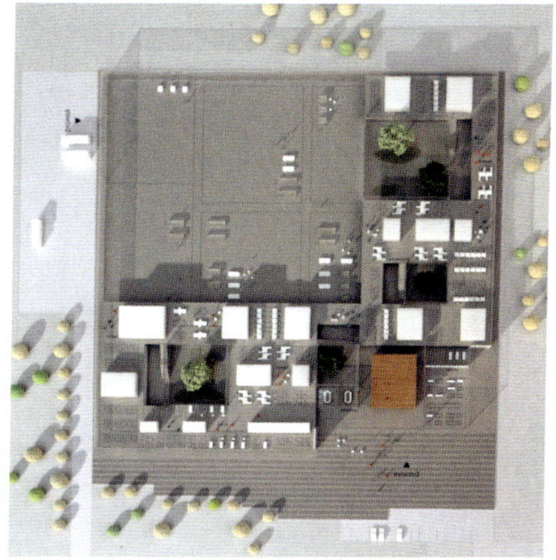

Interdisziplinärer Wissensaustausch: Bürolandschaften und Laborflächen unter einem Dach

Interdisciplinary exchange: Office spaces and laboratories under one roof

Die Räume des 133 Meter langen Gebäudes sind auf quadratischem Grundriss organisiert. Sie gruppieren sich auf zwei Geschossen um vier Innenhöfe, die das Tageslicht nach Innen lenken. Die einzelnen Kompetenzzentren sind als offene Bürolandschaften mit optimierten Cubicles konzipiert. Die Arbeitsplätze verteilen sich in L-Form um die Laborflächen und erleichtern so die direkte Kommunikation zwischen den Mitarbeitern. Lufträume mit offenen Treppen und Kommunikationszonen vernetzen die einzelnen Bereiche und unterstützen den Wissensaustausch der Ingenieure. Der repräsentative Eingang im Süden empfängt Besucher und Mitarbeiter in einer hellen zweigeschossigen Halle. An die zentrale Aula, die für Veranstaltungen und Mitarbeiterversammlungen genutzt wird, schließt im Westen die Cafeteria an. Ihre Außenterrasse ist durch das große auskragende Dach des Gebäudes geschützt. Baubeginn für das Research and Development Centre ist im Frühjahr 2016, die Fertigstellung ist 2017 geplant.

The space in the 133 metre long building is organised on a rectangular shape in plan and grouped on two storeys around four internal courtyards, which direct daylight into the interior of the building. The individual competence centres are designed as open-plan office landscapes with improved office cubicles, which are disposed in an L-shape around the laboratory areas, thereby facilitating direct communication between the employees. Air spaces with open staircases and communications zones interlink the individual areas and promote the exchange of knowledge between engineers. The corporate entrance on the south side invites visitors and employees into a light, bright two-storey hall. The central assembly hall, used for exhibitions and employee meetings, connects to the cafeteria in the west. Its outdoor terrace is sheltered by the building's large roof projection. The Research and Development Center is due to begin construction in spring 2016 and is scheduled for completion in 2017.

1 Laborfläche
2 Bürofläche
3 Gemeinschaftsfläche
4 Innenhof

1 Laboratories
2 Offices
3 Common space
4 Courtyard

Robert Koch-Institut, Haus 6

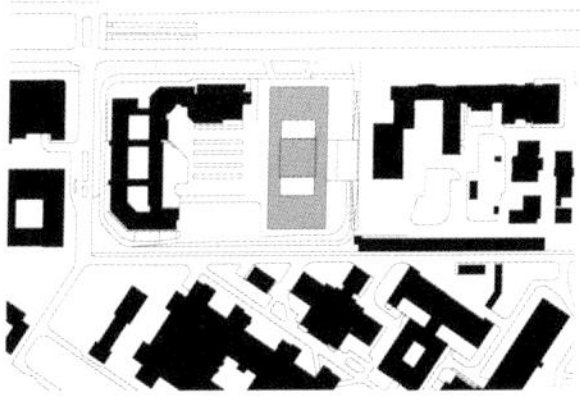

Bundesrepublik Deutschland, vertreten durch das Bundesministerium für Umwelt, Naturschutz, Bau- und Reaktorsicherheit, vertreten durch das Bundesamt für Bauwesen und Raumordnung
Berlin
2005 – 2015

Tragwerksplaner
Krone, Berlin
Technische Ausrüstung
Weber & Partner, Köln
Laborplaner
eretec, Gummersbach
Bauphysik
Müller-BBM, Planegg
Fassadenplaner
Priedemann, Berlin
Landschaftsplaner
Landschaft planen + bauen, Berlin
Brandschutz
HHP Süd, Ludwigshafen
SiGeKo
DEKRA Industrial, Berlin

Im Neubau des Robert Koch-Instituts in Berlin-Wedding befindet sich ein Hochsicherheitslabor der Kategorie S4. Die aerosol- und luftdichten Räume, in denen Wissenschaftler hochpathogene Erreger wie zum Beispiel Ebola- oder Lassaviren erforschen, sind durch mehrstufige Sicherheitssysteme abgeschirmt. Sie liegen in einem würfelförmigen Betonbaukörper, der das Zentrum des neuen Forschungsgebäudes bildet. Innenhöfe und mehrstufige Schleusen separieren das Labor der höchsten Sicherheitskategorie vom übrigen Forschungsgebäude. Die Sicherheitstechnik für das S4-Labor befindet sich in den Geschossen über und unter seinen Räumen in der zweiten Etage. Sie garantiert unter anderem, dass weder Luft noch Abwasser ungefiltert nach außen dringen kann.
Insgesamt stellt das neue Forschungsgebäude des Robert Koch-Instituts 22.000 m^2 Fläche für Labore sowie Büros und Besprechungsräume zur Verfügung. In unmittelbarer Nähe zum Virchow Klinikum sowie zur Sonderisolierstation der Charité und zum Deutschen Herzzentrum ist der Neubau ein wesentlicher Baustein für

The new Robert Koch Institute Building in Berlin-Wedding contains a high-security Biosafety Level 4 Laboratory. The aerosol and air-tight rooms, in which scientists carry out research into highly pathogenic agents such as Ebola and Lassa fever, are shielded by multi-level security systems. The rooms are located in a cube-shaped concrete construction which forms the centre of the new research building. Inner courtyards and pass-through chambers separate the BSL4 Laboratory from the other research buildings. The safety technology for this laboratory is located in the floors above and below its rooms on the second floor and guarantees, among other things, that neither air nor waste water can pass unfiltered out into the environment.
All together, this offers 22,000 m^2 of space for laboratories, offices and meeting rooms. In the direct vicinity of Virchow Hospital, the Charité University Hospital's special isolation centre and the German Heart Institute, the new building is a major component for the infrastructure of the Robert Koch Institute. The building brings all the Berlin facilities of this

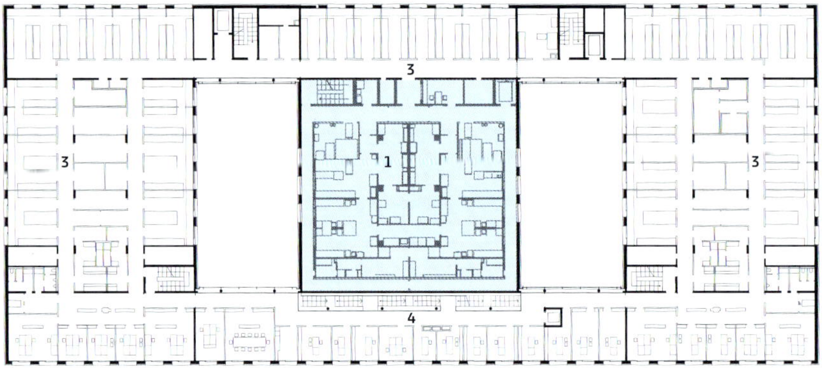

Grundriss 2. Obergeschoss und Längsschnitt

1 S4-Labor
2 S3 Labore
3 S2 Labor
4 Büros
5 Technik

Second floor and longitudinal section

1 Biosafety Level 4 Laboratory
2 Biosafety Level 3 Laboratory
3 Biosafety Level 2 Laboratory
4 Offices
5 Building services

die Infrastruktur des Robert Koch-Instituts. Er konzentriert die Berliner Einrichtungen des renommierten Bundesinstituts am Standort Seestraße.
Die rote Ziegelfassade des langgestreckten Quaders greift das Erscheinungsbild der umliegenden Nachbargebäude auf. Mit einem zentralen Eingangsbereich an der Längsseite orientiert sich das Gebäude zum angrenzenden Campus. Die zweigeschossige Erschließungshalle bildet ein großzügiges Entrée, das sich mit durchgängiger Verglasung nach außen öffnet und gleichzeitig den Blick auf die beiden seitlichen Innenhöfe freigibt, zwischen denen der abgeschirmte Baukörper des Hochsicherheitslabors liegt. Die Büro- und Besprechungsräume des Instituts orientieren sich Richtung Westen zum Campus. An den Innenhöfen und entlang der Außenseiten des Baukörpers reihen sich die Standardlabore auf, ergänzt durch innenliegende Servicebereiche.

renowned national institute together onto the Seestrasse site.
The red brick façade of the elongated cube continues the appearance of the surrounding buildings. With a central entrance area on its longer side, the building is oriented towards the adjacent campus. The two-storey circulation foyer creates a spacious entrance with continuous glazing, which opens to the outside world, while providing views of the internal courtyards on either side.
The Institute's offices and meeting rooms face west towards the campus. Standard laboratories are arranged around the inner courtyards and along the outside of the building, supplemented with the internal service areas.

S4-Labor im 2.Obergeschoss

BSL4 laboratory on the 2nd floor

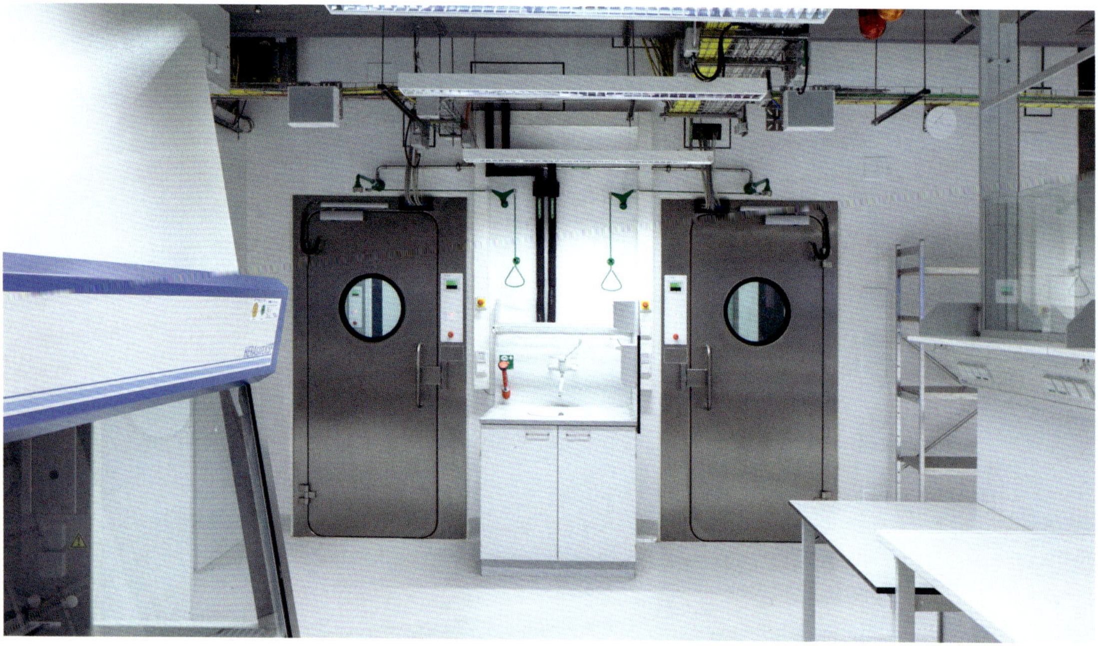

S06.C.02.070a
S4-LABOR 1.1

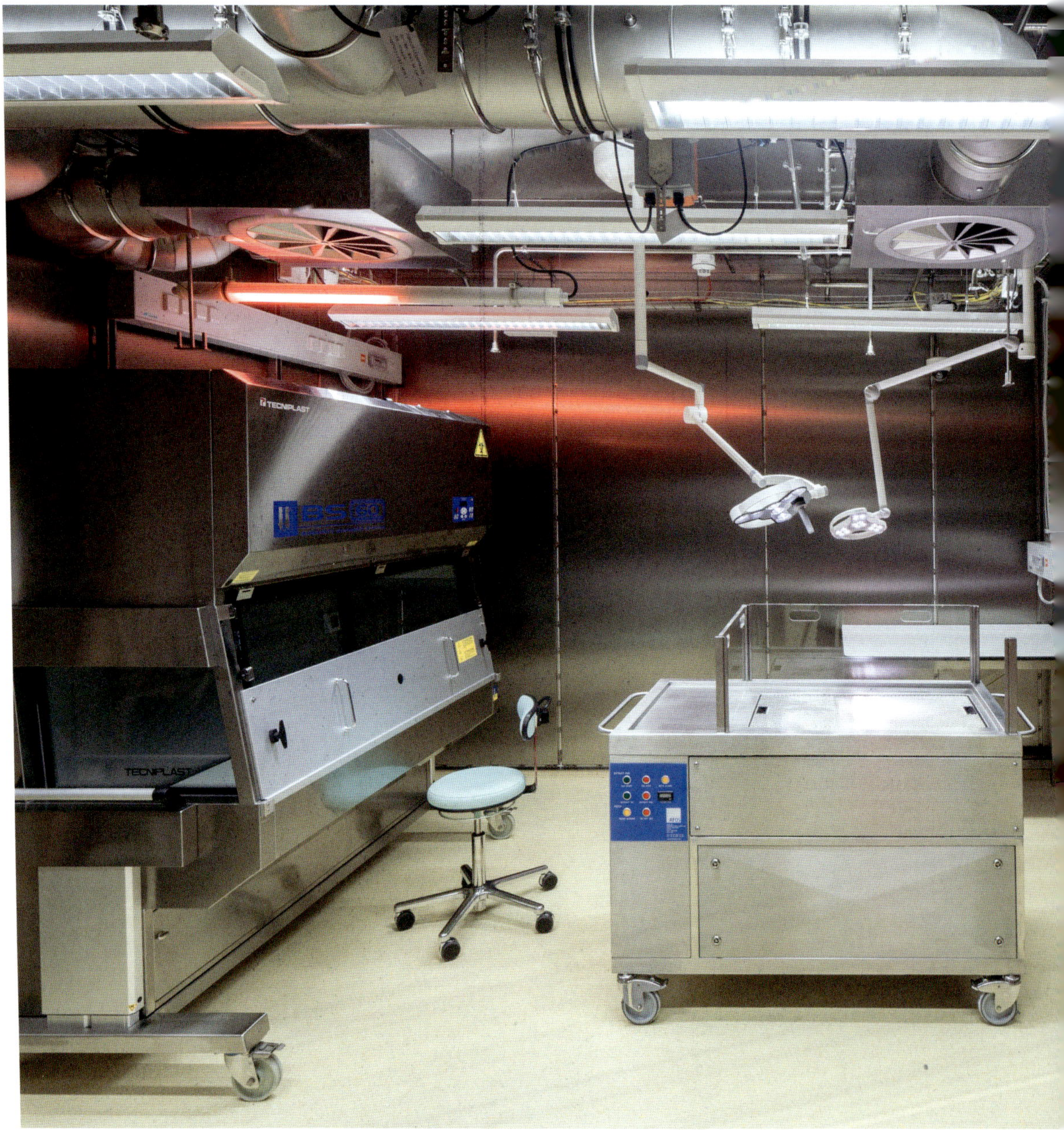
TECNIPLAST
TECNIPLAST

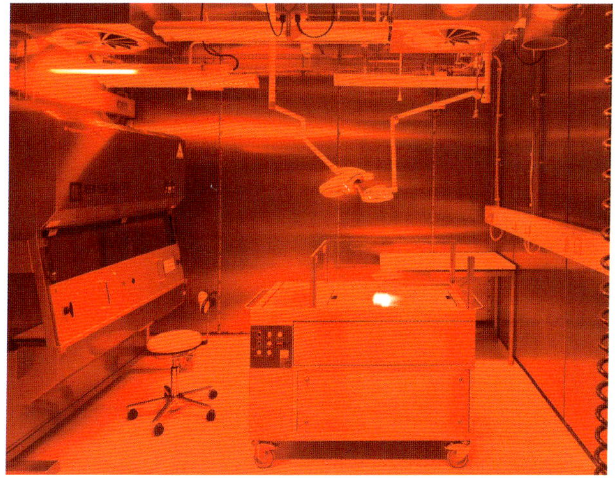

S4-Forschungslabor mit höchsten Sicherheitsanforderungen

The BSL4 Laboratory, with the highest safety requirements

Die Klinkerfassaden binden das Robert Koch-Institut in die Umgebung ein. Sichtbeton umfasst den innenliegenden S4-Baukörper.

The brick-faced Robert Koch Institute blends into the environment. The internal BSL4-cube is clad with exposed concrete.

Fraunhofer

Fraunhofer Pavillon mit Mitarbeiterrestaurant

Fraunhofer-Gesellschaft
Zentralverwaltung
München
2015 - 2017

Technische Ausrüstung
Ingo Geib, München
Tragwerksplaner
Sailer Stepan und Partner, München
Küchenplaner
planungsbüro balke, München

Machbarkeitsstudie
Feasibility study

Da die Zahl der Mitarbeiter in der Zentralverwaltung der Fraunhofer-Gesellschaft in München in den letzten Jahren deutlich gestiegen ist, müssen die Flächen der Kantine und des Konferenzbereichs erweitert werden. Bislang wurden im Mitarbeiterrestaurant in der Hansastraße pro Tag bis zu 400 Essen ausgegeben, in Zukunft soll die Kapazität auf 750 Essen ausgebaut werden.
Nach der Prüfung mehrerer Varianten kommt die Machbarkeitsstudie zu dem Ergebnis, einen Kantinenneubau in den Innenhof der 2002 fertiggestellten Zentralverwaltung zu platzieren. Der zweigeschossige Pavillon mit einer Grundfläche von 400 m² liegt über der Tiefgarage und zeichnet sich durch seine klaren Proportionen und reduzierte Form aus. Die Längsseiten des Baukörpers sind durchgängig verglast, wobei durch den Rücksprung der Fensterflächen ein umlaufender Rahmen entsteht. Die Schmalseiten hingegen sind geschlossen und sollen ebenso wie das Dach begrünt werden. Durch seine leicht versetzte Position zum Zentralgebäude ist der Neubau auch von der Straßenseite aus sichtbar.

As the number of employees at the Fraunhofer Society's central administration building in Munich has significantly increased in recent years, the canteen and conference areas need to be expanded. Until now, up to 400 meals a day were served in the staff restaurant in Hansastrasse. In the future, capacity is to be increased to 750 meals.
After examining several options, it was decided, based on the results of the feasibility analysis, to construct a new canteen in the inner courtyard of the central administration building, which was designed in 2002. The two-storey pavilion with a surface area of 400 m² is situated above the underground car park and is characterised by its clear-cut proportions and concentrated form. The long sides of the structure are fully glazed, whereby the recessed window surface areas create a circumferential frame. The closed narrow sides, on the other hand, together with the roof, will be planted with greenery. Due to its slightly set-back position from the central building, the new structure is also visible from the road side.

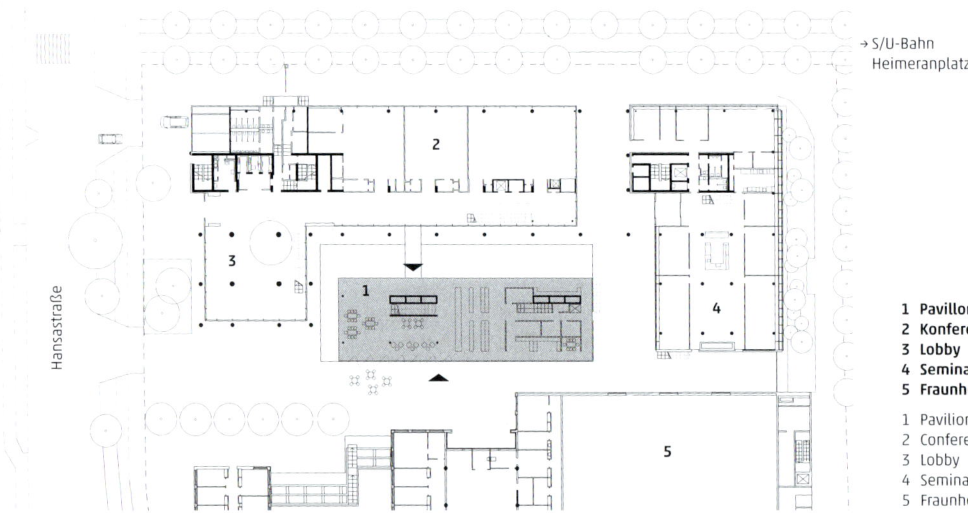

1 Pavillon
2 Konferenzbereich
3 Lobby
4 Seminar
5 Fraunhofer EMFT

1 Pavilion
2 Conference
3 Lobby
4 Seminar
5 Fraunhofer EMFT

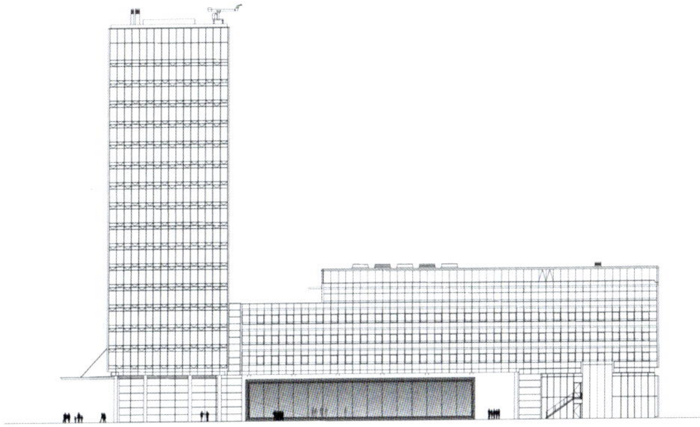

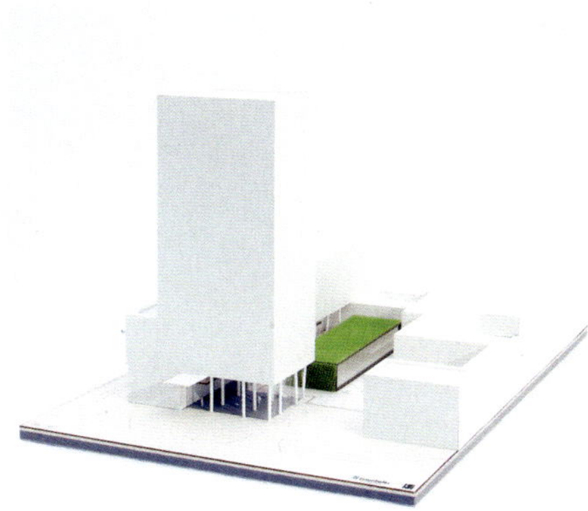

Fraunhofer-Haus
HENN 2002

Der Gastbereich des Mitarbeiterrestaurants ist durch eine Treppe vom Erdgeschoss in das offen gestaltete Obergeschoss erschlossen. Die Nebenräume der Küche werden zum Großteil im Untergeschoss in derzeit als Lagerfläche genutzten Zonen untergebracht.
Nach dem Neubau im Innenhof soll die Bestandsküche im Erdgeschoss der Zentralverwaltung rückgebaut und zu ergänzenden Konferenzflächen umgebaut werden. Da der Umbau in Etappen geplant ist, kann der Kantinenbetrieb während des Bauprozesses aufrechterhalten werden. Die Eröffnung des neuen Mitarbeiterrestaurants ist für 2019 vorgesehen.

The guest area of the staff restaurant is connected by a staircase which runs from the ground floor to the open-plan upper floor. The auxiliary rooms of the kitchen are mainly located in the basement area in zones that are currently used for storage.
Following the completion of the new building in the inner courtyard, the existing kitchen on the ground floor of the central administration building is to be dismantled and converted into supplementary conference space. As this conversion is planned in stages, canteen operations can be maintained during the construction process. The opening of the new staff restaurant is planned for 2019.

Ansicht Innenhof Fraunhofer-Haus mit neuem Pavillon für das Mitarbeiterrestaurant

Elevation courtyard Fraunhofer-House with new pavilion for the staff restaurant

Niedersächsisches Zentrum für Biomedizintechnik, Implantatforschung und Entwicklung

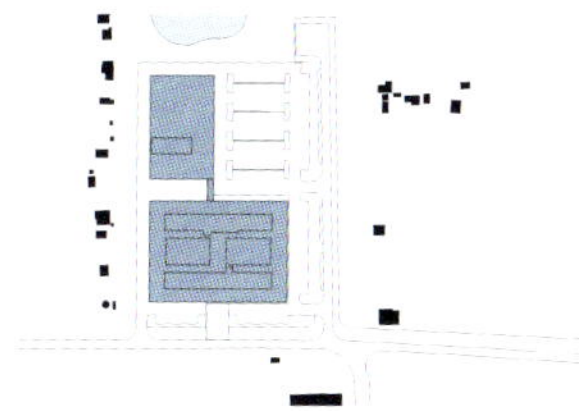

Staatliches Baumanagement Hannover
2012 – 2015

Tragwerksplaner
Assmann, Magdeburg
Technische Ausrüstung
Inros lackner, Rostock
Laborplaner
TEAMPLAN, Tübingen
Bauphysik
m+P, Braunschweig
Elektroplaner
ZWP Ingenieure, Köln
Fassadenplaner
iPb Blei, Gundelfingen
Landschaftsplaner
Inros lackner, Rostock
Brandschutz
IBB, Groß Schwülper

Im Niedersächsischen Zentrum für Biomedizintechnik und Implantatforschung in Hannover (NIFE) befinden sich Büros und Laborräume für vier wissenschafliche Einrichtungen zur Entwicklung medizinischer Implantate in den Bereichen Hören, Neurochirurgie, Herz, Kreislauf, Zahn und Skelettsystem.
Die beiden Neubauten am Rand des Campusgeländes der Medizinischen Hochschule Hannover stellen 17.400 m² Fläche für die vernetzten Arbeitsplätze von bis zu 300 Mitarbeitern bereit. Das dreigeschossige Laborgebäude am Stadtfelddamm und das rückwärtige Tierhaus mit zwei Geschossen sind durch einen Gang miteinander verbunden. Prägendes Element des Entwurfs ist eine durchgängige Magistrale. Die zentrale Erschließungs- und Versorgungsachse betont den Eingangsbereich an der Straßenseite und ermöglicht den Nutzern eine einfache Orientierung im Gebäude. An sie schließen zwei Lichthöfe und die vier Nutzungsbereiche an. Kommunikationsflächen entlang der Achse unterstützen den Wissensaustausch und fördern die transdisziplinäre Zusammenarbeit.

The Lower Saxony Centre for Biomedical Technology, Implant Research and Development in Hanover (NIFE) comprises offices and laboratory rooms for four scientific departments engaged in the development of medical implants in the fields of hearing, neurosurgery, cardiovascular systems, dentistry and orthopaedics.
The two new buildings on the edge of the campus of the Hanover Medical School provide a floor area of 17,400 m² with integrated workplaces for up to 300 employees.
The three-storey laboratory building on Stadtfelddamm and the rearward two-storey animal unit are linked by a walkway. The defining element of the design is a continuous main central axis. This central movement and supply route emphasises the entrance area on the roadside and provides users with a simple means of orientation within the building.
The entrace connects to two light wells and four usage areas. Communication zones along the axis encourage the exchange of knowledge and promote interdisciplinary cooperation.

Stadtfelddamm
Feodor-Lynen-Straße

Zusätzliche öffentliche Bereiche bietet die zweigeschossige Halle in der ersten Etage über der Magistrale. Die verglasten Besprechungs- und Aufenthaltsräume in diesem Bereich schaffen ein kommunikatives Umfeld, das von allen Forschungsgruppen flexibel genutzt werden kann. Um die Lichthöfe und entlang der Außenfassaden gruppieren sich auf den einzelnen Geschossen die Labor- und Büroarbeitsplätze. Nach außen präsentiert sich das Forschungs- und Entwicklungszentrum mit einer dunklen Lochfassade, die mit Faserzementplatten verkleidet ist. Der Neubau ist ein maßgeblicher Baustein für das Exzellenzprofil der Stadt Hannover als Wissenschaftsstandort im Bereich der Medizintechnik.

The two-storey hall offers additional public areas on the first floor via the main axis. The glazed official and informal meeting rooms in this area create a communicative environment that can be used flexibly by all research groups. The laboratories and office workstations are arranged together on the first floor around the light wells and along the external façades. The research and development centre presents a dark perforated façade clad with fibre cement to the outside world. The new building makes an important contribution to Hanover's profile of excellence as a leading centre in the field of medical technology.

Erdgeschoss
Ground floor

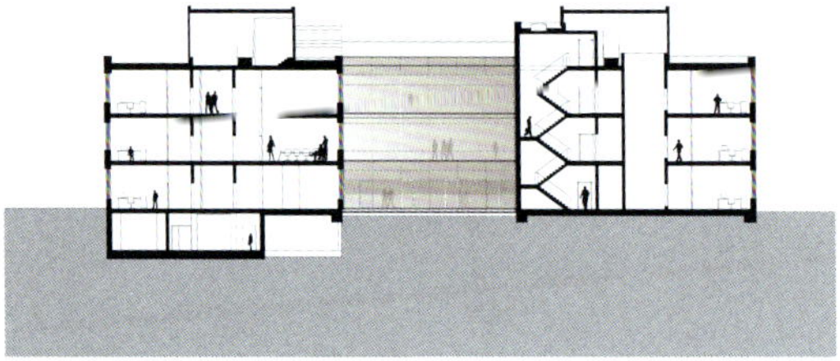

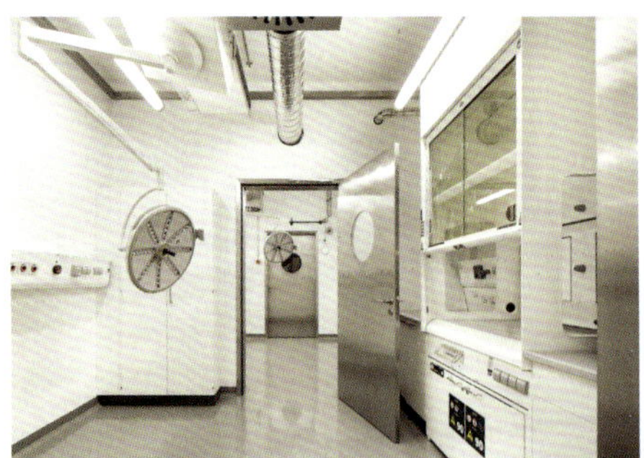

←
Obergeschoss
Labore und Büros sind um die beiden Lichthöfe angeordnet

Upper level
Laboratories and offices are arranged around the open courtyards

Wissenschafts- und Werkstattsgebäude am MLZ

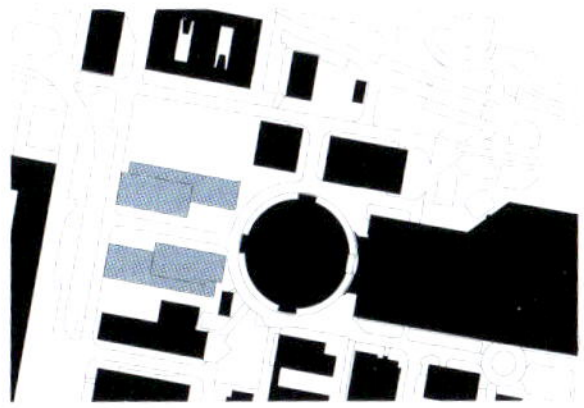

Staatliches Bauamt Rosenheim
Garching
2014 – 2019

Tragwerksplaner
henke rapolder frühe, München
Technische Ausrüstung
Ottitsch, München
Elektrotechnik
Duschl, Rosenheim

Das Heinz Maier-Leibnitz Zentrum (MLZ) mit Blick auf das denkmalgeschützte Atom-Ei

The Heinz Maier-Leibnitz Centre (MLZ) with view to the heritage-listed "Atom-Ei"

Die Forschungs-Neutronenquelle am Forschungsreaktor München II (FRM II) in Garching der Technischen Universität München (TUM) wird wissenschaftlich durch eine Kooperation der TUM mit den Helmholtz Zentren aus Jülich (Forschungszentrum Jülich GmbH, FZJ) und Geesthacht (HZG) genutzt. Zur Erweiterung der Arbeitsflächen für die Wissenschaftler errichten jeweils das FZJ (Wissenschaftsgebäude) und die TUM (Werkstattsgebäude) ein viergeschossiges Gebäude mit insgesamt 9.300 m² Fläche geplant. Die beiden langgestreckten Baukörper liegen westlich des abgeschalteten Forschungsreaktors (1957 – 2000); die Achse zwischen ihnen gibt den Blick auf das denkmalgeschützte Atom-Ei frei.
Versetzte Vor- und Rücksprünge in der Kubatur der Gebäude stellen Bezüge zum jeweiligen Gegenüber her und lassen an ein ineinandergeschobenes Gesamtvolumen denken. Die Gebäudefassaden aus vorgehängten Sichtbetonelementen setzen einen Kontrapunkt zur Metallhülle des Atom-Ei's.

The research neutron source at the Research Reactor Munich II (FRM II) in Garching is used by the Technical University Munich (TUM) and the Jülich Research Institute (FZJ). Two four-storey buildings with a total floor area of 9,300 m² are planned to expand the working quarters for the reactor's researchers. Both elongated buildings lie west of the shut-down research reactor (1957 – 2000). The axis running between them offers a view of the heritage-listed "Atom-Ei".
Staggered projections and recesses in the cubature of the buildings establish a connection with their counterparts and create the impression of an integrated, interlocked single building. The building façades, consisting of fair-faced concrete panel curtain walls, set a contrapuntal tone to the shimmering metal shell of the "Atom-Ei".
The TUM's northern research building contains a large two-storey workshop on its ground and first floors, with the two upper storeys occupied by offices.

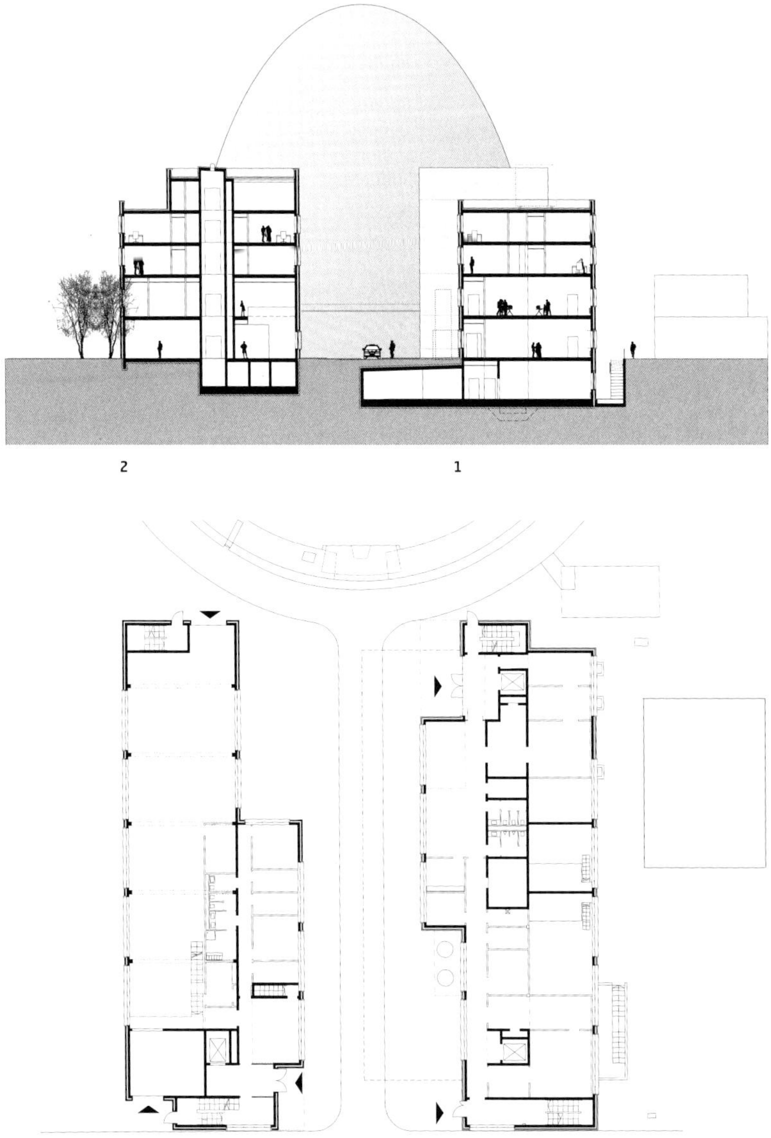

1
Labor- und Bürogebäude des Forschungszentrums Jülich

Laboratory and Office Building of Forschungszentrum Jülich

2
Wissenschafts- und Werkstatt-gebäude der Technischen Universität München

Science and Workshop building of the Technical University Munich

Grundriss und Schnitt

Ground floor and section

Das nördliche Forschungsgebäude der Technischen Universität München fasst in seinem Erdgeschoss und im ersten Stock eine große doppelgeschossige Werkstatt, die beiden oberen Etagen nehmen Büroflächen auf.
In der gegenüberliegenden Außenstelle des Forschungszentrums Jülich sollen Laborflächen für verschiedene Forschungsschwerpunkte Platz finden. Die beiden oberen Stockwerke des Gebäudes werden für Büros genutzt.
Die Technikzentralen sind jeweils integriert, sie befinden sich im fensterlosen Obergeschoss der höheren Gebäudeteile. Treppenhäuser an den Stirnseiten erschließen die Innenräume, zusätzlich sind im dunkleren Mittelbereich Aufzüge platziert. Insgesamt erweitern beide Neubauten die Forschungseinrichtungen am MLZ in Garching mit Flächen für 270 Arbeitsplätze.

The Jülich Research Institute's annex opposite will provide space for laboratories dedicated to various fields of research. The two upper floors of the building are used for offices.
The technical centres are similarly integrated into the windowless upper storeys of the higher parts of the building. Stairways on the back of the building connect the internal spaces, supplemented by lifts in the darker central areas. The two new buildings will add enough space for further 270 workstations.

Vortragssaal im Labor- und Bürogebäude des FZ Jülich

Auditorium in the Lab- and Office building of Forschungszentrum Jülich

attocube systems Unternehmenssitz

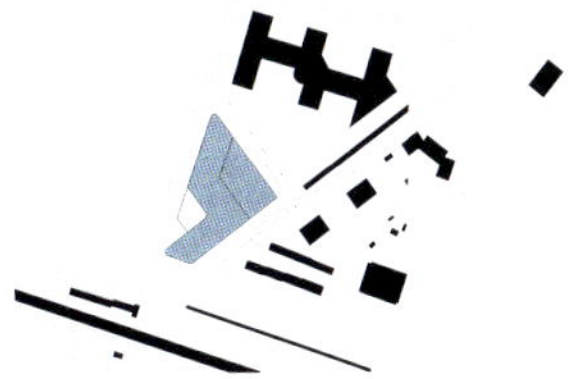

attocube systems AG
München
2015

Das Unsichtbare sichtbar machen, ist das Ziel von attocube systems. Als führendes Unternehmen im Bereich der Mechatronik und Nanotechnologie innoviert, entwickelt und produziert es Mikroskope, Sensoren und Positionierer, die in der Spitzenforschung sowie in der Industrie weltweit zum Einsatz kommen. Mit dem neuen Unternehmenssitz in Haar bei München möchte attocube systems sein erfolgreiches Wachstum abbilden und das erste Firmengebäude seiner jungen Unternehmensgeschichte realisieren. Im Rahmen des Programmings wurden zunächst die Prozesse des Technologieunternehmens und die vielfältigen Interaktionspunkte seiner Forschung, Entwicklung und Produktion analysiert. Die erfasste enge Vernetzung der Bereiche sowie die Verzahnung mit der Öffentlichkeit und der weltweiten Forschungswelt entsprechen dem Selbstverständnis von Transparenz und Offenheit. Als Basis und Anker für diesen Thinkspace ist die Produktion der Nano-Manufaktur anzusehen, in der mit höchster Konzentration und Präzision Entwicklungen realisiert werden.

"Making the invisible visible" is the objective of attocube systems. As a leading company in the field of mechatronics and nanotechnology, the company innovates, develops and manufactures microscopes, sensors and positioners, which are used worldwide in cutting-edge research and industry. With its new headquarters in Haar near Munich, attocube systems plans to continue its successful growth and to realise the first new building in the company's young history. Initially, as part of its programming process, the technology company's procedures and the multifaceted points of interaction of its research, development and production were analysed.
The analysed close interconnection of the areas as well as communication with the public and the global research world correspond to the company's self-perception of transparency and openness. Nanomanufacturing can be regarded as the basis and anchor for this thinkspace, in which developments are implemented with maximum concentration and precision.

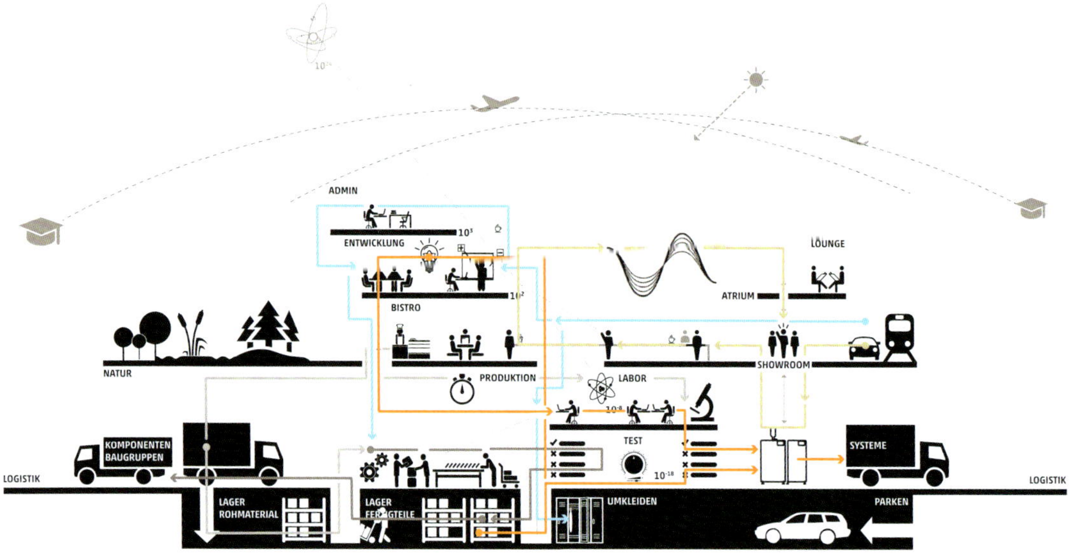

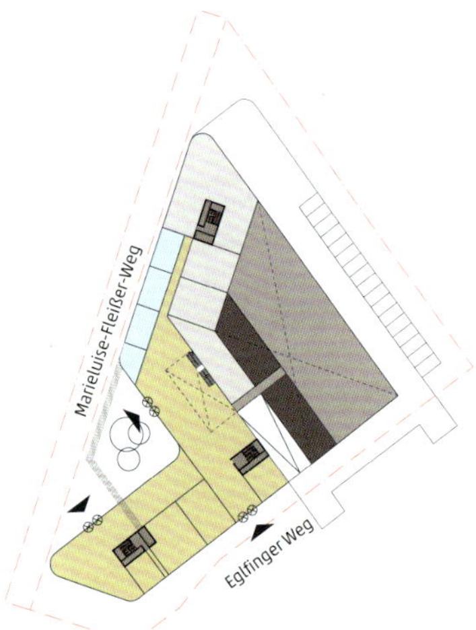

Erdgeschoss
Produktion / Logistik
Foyer / Caféteria

Ground floor
Production / Logistics
Foyer / Caféteria

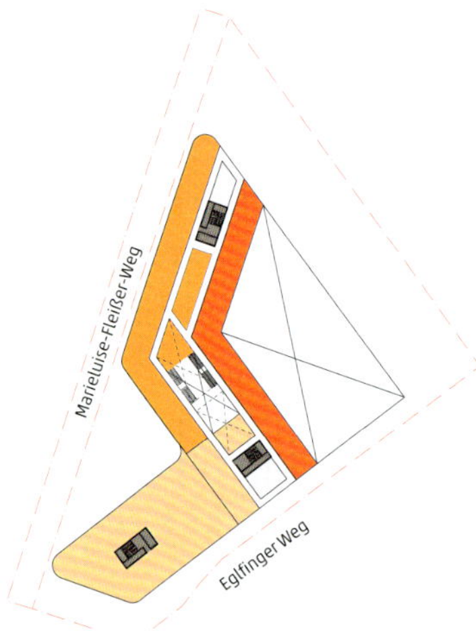

1. Obergeschoss
Entwicklung

First floor
Development

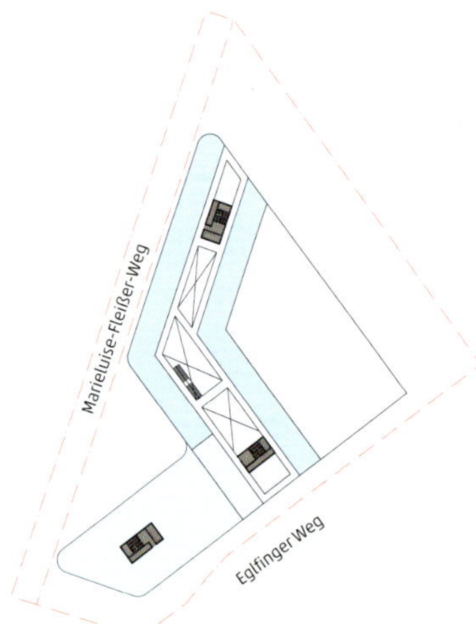

2. Obergeschoss
Verwaltung

Second floor
Administration

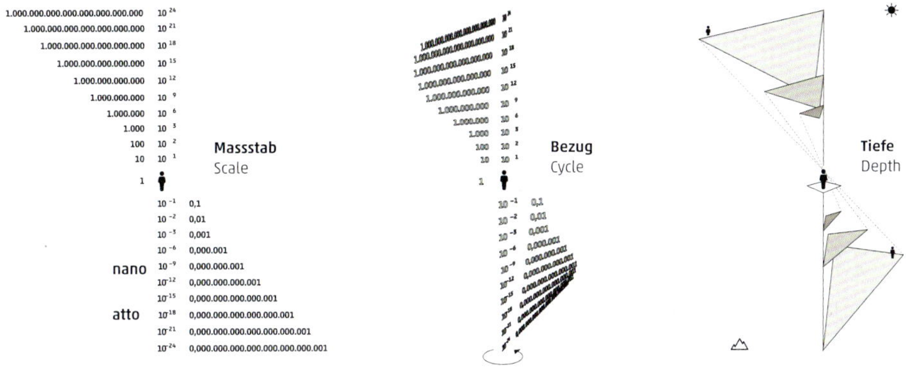

Ein Attometer (am) entspricht einem milliardstel Nanometer (nm)

An attometre (am) equals one-billionth of a nanometre (nm)

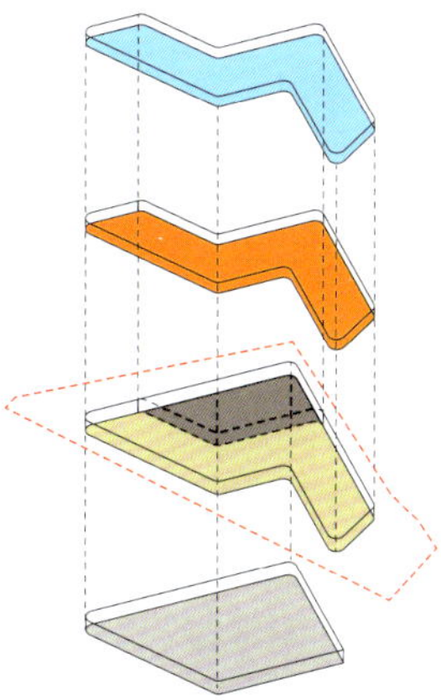

In einem zweiten Schritt des Programmings wurde ein räumliches Konzept entwickelt, das den ermittelten Flächenbedarf in transparente und offene interdisziplinäre Bereiche sowie disziplinäre Bereiche für die Konzentration und Präzision anordnet. In dem so geschaffenen Spannungsraum bewegen sich Mitarbeiter, Kunden und die Öffentlichkeit. Im Erdgeschoss des geschwungenen Firmengebäudes liegen das Café, die Konferenzräume, ein Showroom sowie die nach Norden orientierte Produktion mit Lagerflächen und einer Anlieferzone. Die beiden Obergeschosse sind der Entwicklung mit Laboren und Büros gewidmet, die über Atrien sowohl untereinander als auch mit der Produktion vernetzt sind.

In a second programming step, a spatial concept was developed, which serves to organise the specified surface area requirements into transparent and open interdisciplinary zones as well as disciplinary areas for concentration and precision. Employees, clients and the public converge in this highly-energised sphere. The café, conference rooms, a showroom as well as the northerly-oriented production facilities with warehousing space and a delivery zone, will be included on the ground floor of the curved company building. The two upper floors are dedicated to development with laboratories and offices and are connected by atria with each other and with the production area.

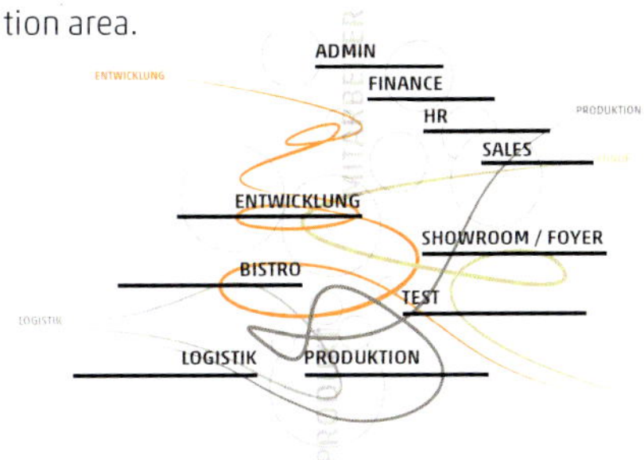

Wettbewerbe 2015
Competitions 2015

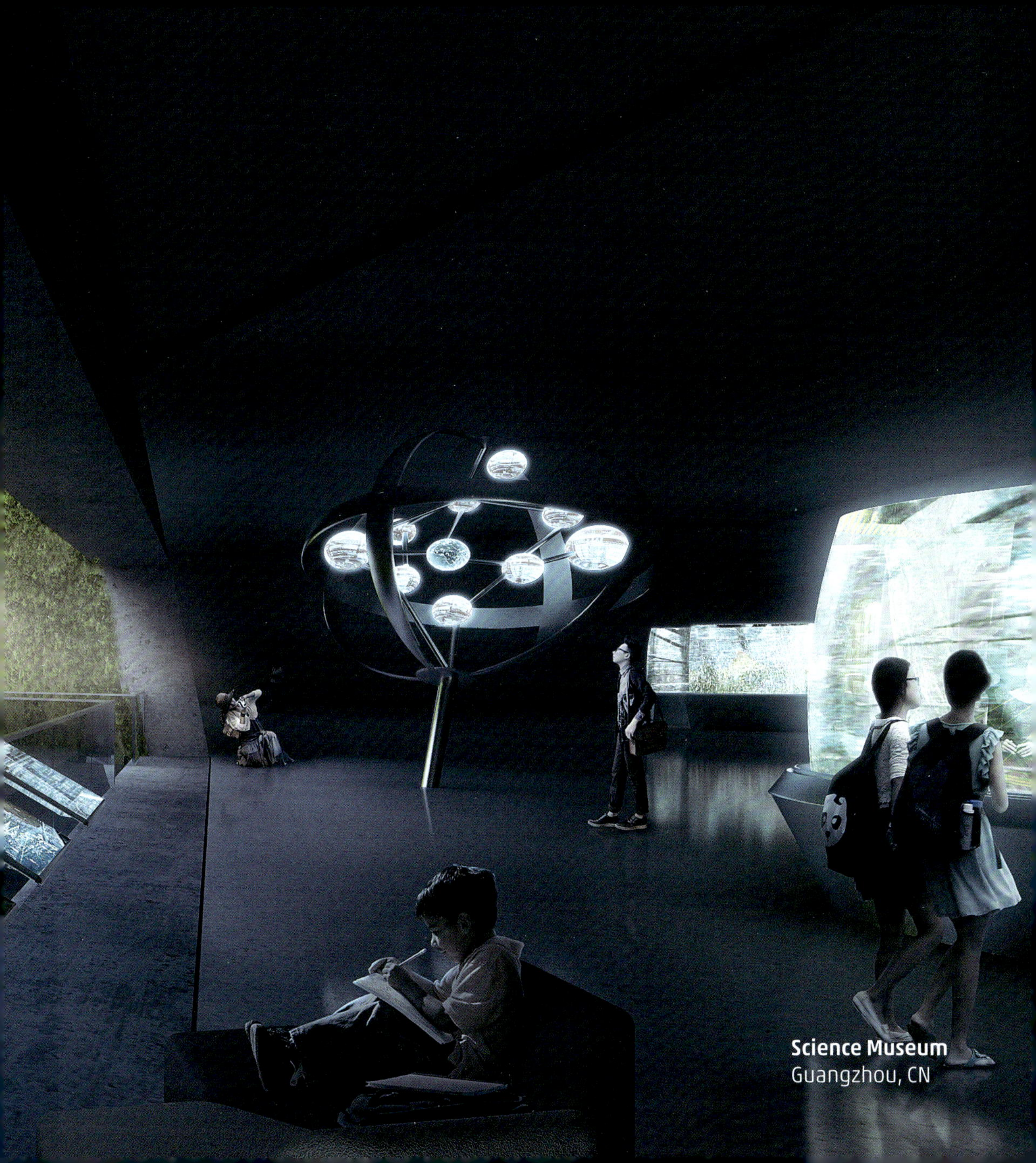

Science Museum
Guangzhou, CN

Fakultät für Social Sciences

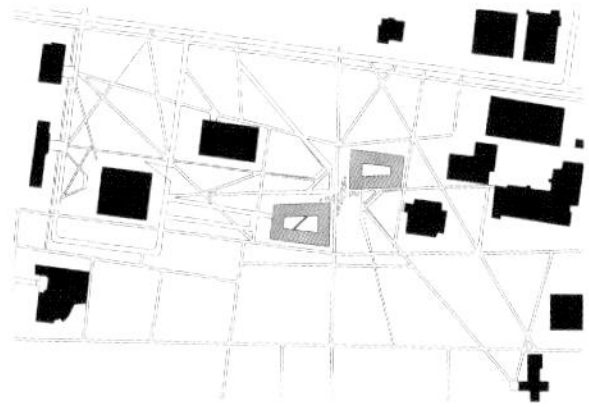

Radboud University
Nijmegen, Holland
2015

Lokaler Planungspartner
RAU, Amsterdam

Wettbewerb 2015
Competition 2015

Der zentrumsnahe Campus der Radboud University im niederländischen Nimwegen ist in einen historischen Park eingebettet. Der Wettbewerbsentwurf für das neue Fakultätsgebäude mit Instituten und Forschungseinrichtungen knüpft an die offene und transparente Formensprache der Bestandsarchitektur des Campus an. Er greift ihre zurückhaltende Gestik auf und bindet sie in ein landschaftsarchitektonisches Konzept ein, das die Sichtachsen innerhalb des Campus verstärkt und Verbindungswege zwischen den einzelnen Gebäuden schafft. Geplant sind zwei freistehende Gebäudekörper auf orthogonalem Grundriss, die über eine eingeschossige öffentliche Halle auf Erdgeschossniveau miteinander verbunden sind. Ihre Fassaden sind an den Achsen des Campusareals ausgerichtet und je nach Sonneneinstrahlung und Lage durchgängig verglast oder mit vertikalen Glas- und Stahllamellen ausgestattet.
Skulpturale Treppen erschließen die beiden Gebäude mit jeweils eigenem Atrium, das optische Verbindungen zu seinem Gegenüber herstellt.

The centrally-located campus of Radboud University in Nijmegen in the Netherlands is embedded in a historic park. The competition design for the new faculty building connects with the open and transparent stylistic idiom of the existing campus architecture, taking up its cautious gestures and integrating these in a concept of architectural landscape that strengthens the visual axes within the campus and creates connecting paths between the individual buildings. Two freestanding structures on an orthogonal ground plan are envisaged, linked to one another by a single storey public hall at ground floor level. The façades are oriented towards the campus area axes and are fully glazed or fitted with vertical glass and steel slats according to sun intensity and position. Sculptural stairways provide access to both buildings, each with their own atrium which establishes a visual connection with each other.
The floor space of the reinforced concrete construction is modularly subdivided, thus allowing flexible utilisation which can be modified to suit with future requirements.

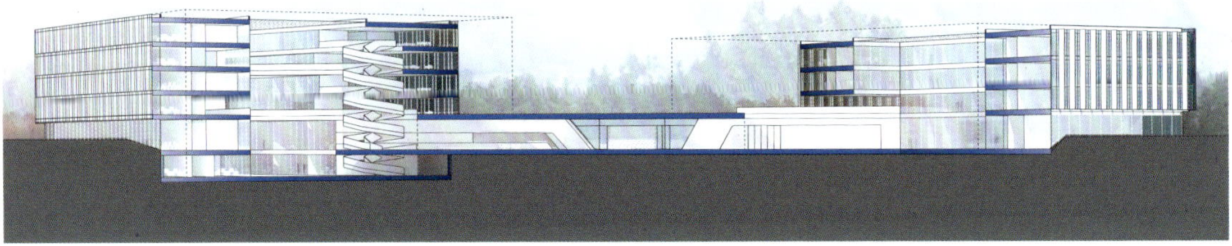

Der zentrale Zugang im Park verbindet beide Institutsgebäude

The central entrance, located in the park, connects both institutes

Die Geschossflächen des Stahlbetonbaus sind modular unterteilt und erlauben eine flexible Nutzung, die an zukünftige Anforderungen angepasst werden kann. Alle Gemeinschaftsfunktionen des Fakultätsgebäudes wie das Auditorium, die Konferenzräume und Garderoben gruppieren sich um die zentrale Eingangshalle, über die sich die angehobene Parklandschaft wölbt. Das Café öffnet sich mit bodentiefen Fenstern ins Grüne und auf den zentralen Vorplatz des Haupteingangs.

All communal functions of the faculty building such as the auditorium, conference rooms and cloakrooms are grouped around a central entrance hall, with the elevated park landscape arching above. With its floor-to-ceiling windows, the café opens onto the green landscape and the central forecourt of the main entrance.

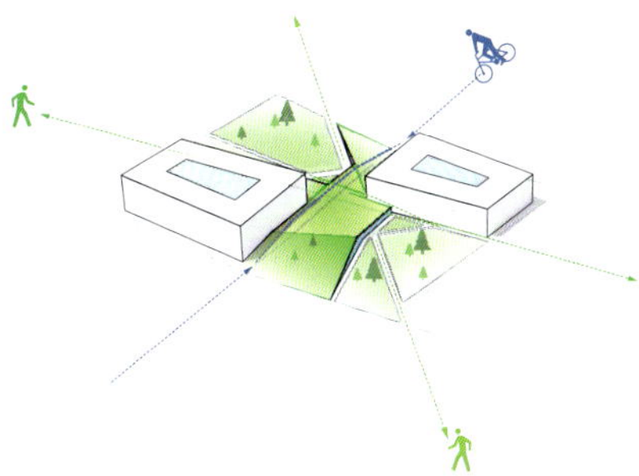

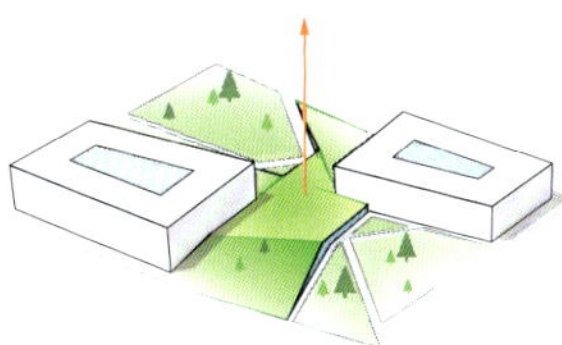

Besucher- und Informationszentrum Nationalpark Schwarzwald

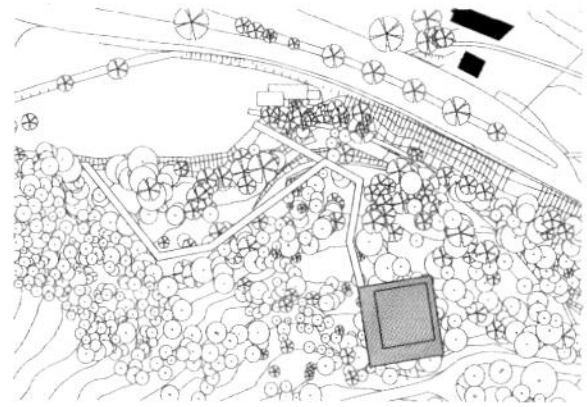

Vermögen und Bau Baden-Württemberg, Pforzheim
Seebach, Baiersbronn am Ruhestein
2015

Technische Ausrüstung
Süss Beratende Ingenieure, München
Tragwerksplaner
merz kley partner, Dornbirn
Landschaftsplaner
Nowak Landschaftsarchitekten, München

Wettbewerb 2015
Ankauf

Competition 2015
Purchase

Die sensible Verbindung von Mensch und Natur steht im Zentrum des Entwurfs für das Besucherzentrum Nationalpark Schwarzwald. Der Wald ist Leitthema für ein sinnliches Erlebnis, dessen gezielte Wahrnehmung von der Architektur unterstützt wird. Das Besucherzentrum ist als vertikaler Solitär umgeben von Bäumen konzipiert. Seine Nutzungen sind auf sieben Geschosse mit quadratischem Grundriss verteilt. Neben 3.800 m² Ausstellungsfläche befinden sich in dem kompakten Gebäude Räume für Vorträge und Filmvorführungen sowie für Gastronomie und Verwaltung.
Holzmaserungen, die sich wie ein Fingerabdruck auf den Betonfassaden des Gebäudes abzeichnen, prägen sein Erscheinungsbild. Durch große Einschnitte und Öffnungen wird der Monolith aus Beton zu einer abstrakten Skulptur, die in Kontrast zu ihrem grünen Umfeld steht und gleichzeitig den Dialog mit der Natur aufnimmt. Vom höher gelegenen Parkplatz führt ein Steg durch die Baumwipfel des Waldes zum Foyer im zweiten Stockwerk des Ausstellungsgebäudes. Der Weg dorthin ist als Lehrpfad angelegt, der die Besucher auf das

The sensory connection of people and nature lies at the heart of the design for the Black Forest National Park Visitor Centre. The forest is the leading theme for a sensory experience, the specific perception of which is supported by the architecture.
The visitor centre is a vertical stand-alone structure surrounded by trees. The rectangular floors on its seven storeys are all used for visitor centre purposes. In addition to 3,800 m² of exhibition space, the compact building houses rooms for presentations and film screenings, catering and administration.
Wood grain, which can be seen like a finger print on the concrete façade of the building, defines its appearance. With deep incisions and openings, the concrete monolith becomes an abstract sculpture which stands in contrast to its green surroundings, while still entering a dialogue with nature.
A tree-top path leads from the higher-level car park through to the foyer on the second floor of the exhibition building. The path takes the form of a nature trail so that visitors can become familiar with the subject. From the

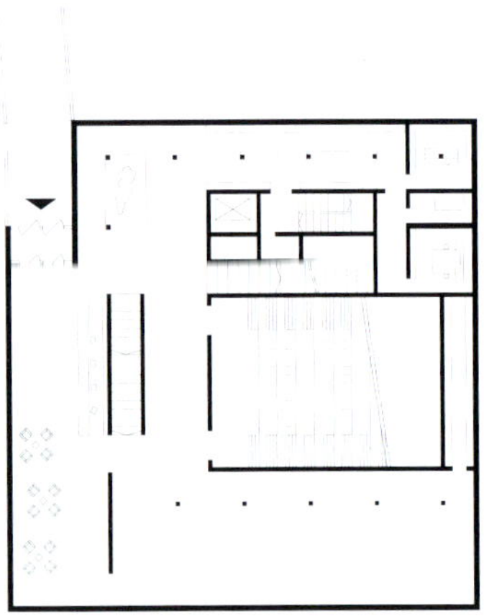

2. Obergeschoss
Second floor

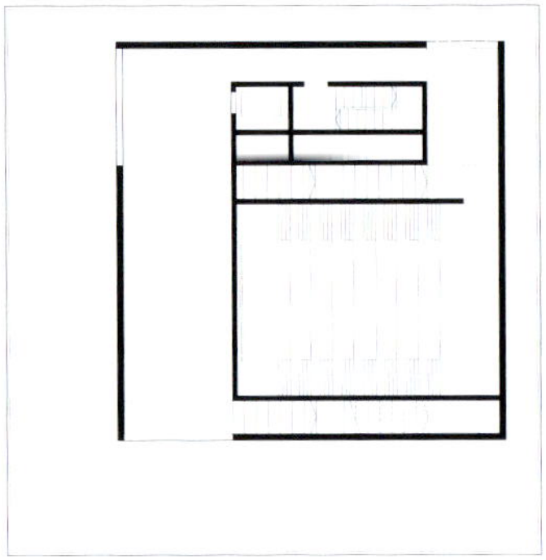

3. Obergeschoss
Third floor

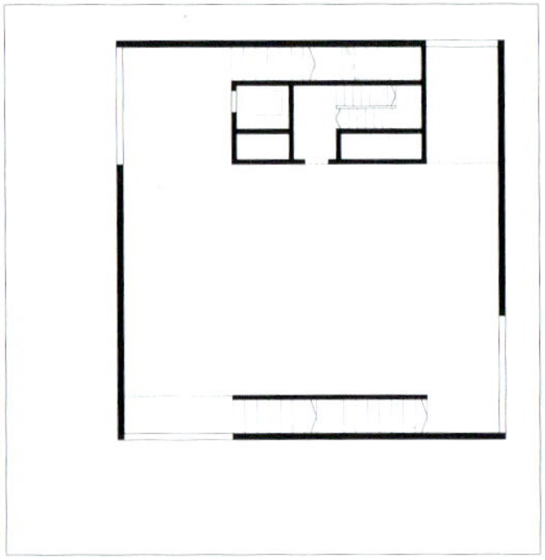

4. Obergeschoss
Fourth floor

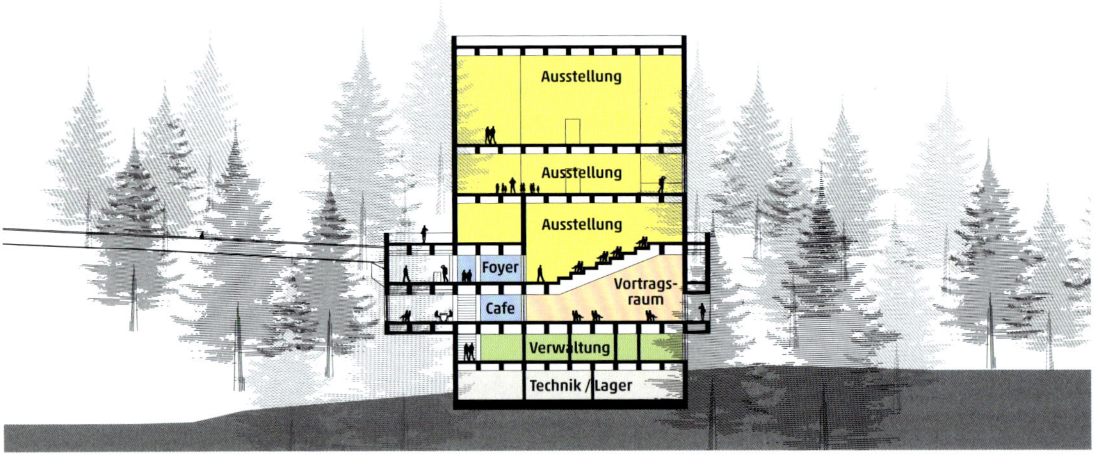

Thema einstimmt. Vom Eingangsbereich wird der Blick durch zwei große, in Holz gerahmte Fenster auf den umliegenden Wald gelenkt. In fließenden Übergängen werden die Räume für die Wechselausstellungen und der Kinosaal erschlossen. Die Dauerausstellung in den Obergeschossen schließt mit einem Raum der Stille ab, der die Sinne auf die Erfahrung der Natur konzentriert. Das Ausstellungskonzept vermittelt Hintergrundinformationen sowie Forschungszusammenhänge zum Thema Wald. Es veranschaulicht sie mit virtuellen und realen, digitalen und emotional inszenierten Bereichen. Fensterflächen entlang der Außenwände stellen wie große Schaufenster eine Verbindung zur Natur her und lenken die Aufmerksamkeit auf den Wald. Sein Klima und seine Geräuschkulisse werden auf einer umlaufenden Terrasse im dritten Obergeschoss ins Zentrum der Wahrnehmung gerückt.

entrance area, the visitor's gaze is directed through two large windows framed in wood towards the surrounding forest. The rooms transition smoothly into the temporary exhibition area and the cinema hall. The permanent exhibition on the upper floors terminates with a peaceful space that focuses the visitor's attention on experiencing nature. The exhibition concept provides background information and details of research on forests. It displays them in virtual and real, digital and emotive presentational environments. Windows along the external walls produce an effect like large display windows, creating a connection with nature and directing attention towards the forest. Climate and background noise are set centre stage on a continuous terrace on the third floor.

Über die Baumwipfel ragt das Besucherzentrum, die Brücke zum Eingang verläuft durch die Baumkronen

The visitor centre juts out over the treetops; an elevated runway leads through the forest to the main entrance

Helmholtz Zentrum für Umweltforschung

Helmholtz Zentrum UFZ
Leipzig
2015

Tragwerksplaner
bwp Burggraf + Reiminger, München
Technische Ausrüstung
Süss Beratende Ingenieure, München
Laborplaner
dr. heinekamp, Karlsfeld
Landschaftsplaner
Rainer Schmidt, München
Brandschutz
Gruner, Stuttgart

Wettbewerb 2015
Competition 2015

Das Forschungsgebäude auf dem Campus des Umweltforschungszentrums Helmholtz in Leipzig (UFZ) ist als freistehendes Hochhaus konzipiert. Der Entwurf gliedert den Baukörper horizontal in zwei Einheiten und macht somit die Funktionseinteilung zwischen den beiden Departments Solare Materialien (SoMa) und Ökologische Toxikologie (Ökotox) nach außen sichtbar.
Die Innenräume des Neubaus stellen vielfältige Räume für die Konzentration und Kommunikation, die Forschung und den Wissensaustausch zur Verfügung und vernetzen die einzelnen Bereiche miteinander. In jeder Etage befinden sich Labore und Büros sowie eine wechselnde Zahl an Denkzellen, die durch Kommunikations- und Sozialflächen miteinander verbunden sind. Das dritte Geschoss wird als zentrale Kommunikationsebene mit Vortrags- und Besprechungsflächen gemeinsam genutzt. Es bildet eine Zäsur zwischen den beiden Departments in den oberen und unteren Etagen. Nach außen zeichnet sich dieser Einschnitt durch den Rücksprung im Fassadenbild ab.

The research building on the Helmholtz Environmental Research Centre (UFZ) campus in Leipzig is designed as a free-standing high-rise building. The design concept divides the building horizontally into two components, making the functional division between the two departments, Solar Materials (SoMa) and Ecological Toxicology (Ökotox) visible from the outside.
The inside of the building provides versatile spaces for concentration and communication, research and knowledge exchange while connecting the individual areas with each other. Laboratories and offices as well as an increasing number of thinking cells which are connected with each other by communication and social areas are located on each floor. The third floor is used as a main communications floor with rooms for lectures and meetings. It forms a buffer between the two departments in the upper and lower floors. From the outside, this floor can be recognised by its recessed façade.

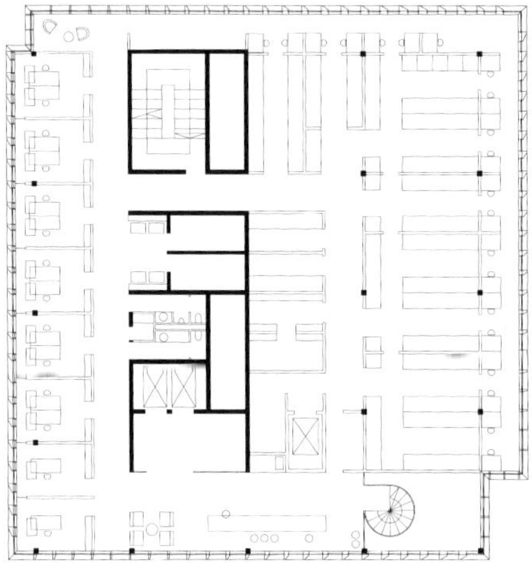

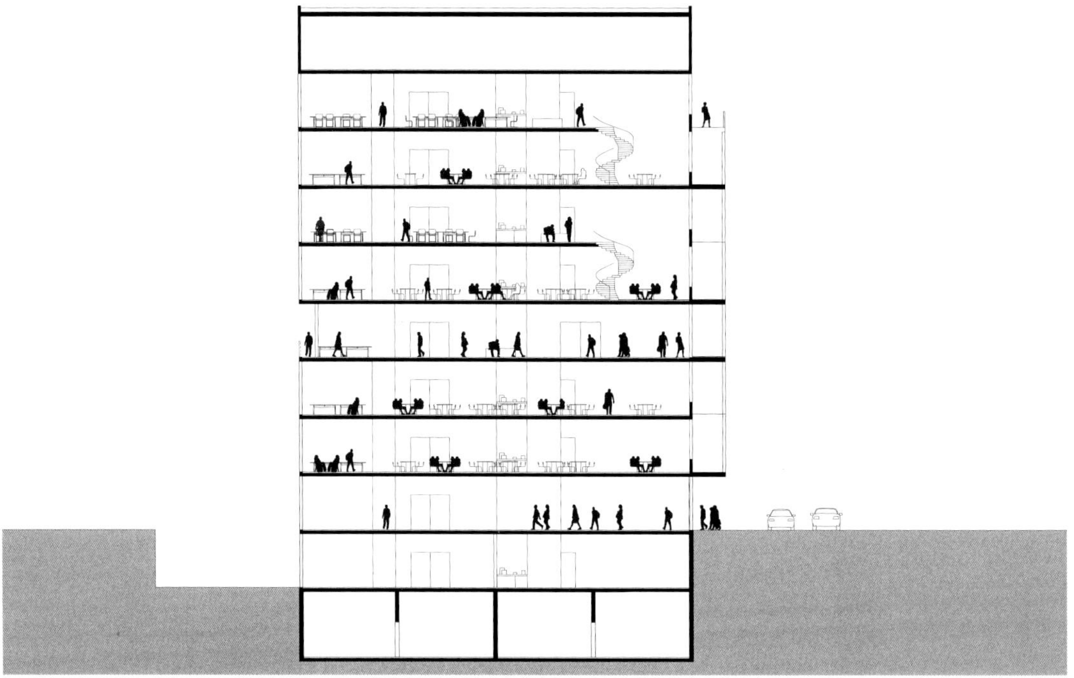

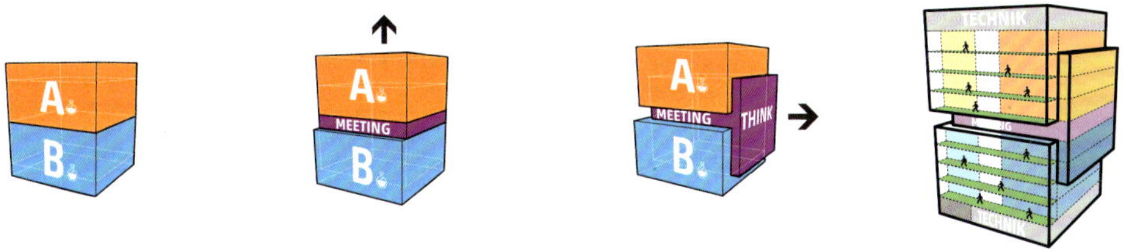

Departments Meeting Think Function

↗
Konzept
Volumen und Funktionen

Concept
Volumes and functions

Die einzelnen Geschosse und Departments sind durch ein klares Kommunikations- und Erschließungsprinzip miteinander verbunden. Ihre Interaktion wird durch eine Wendeltreppe gestärkt, die als Begegnungsraum konzipiert ist und sämtliche Geschosse miteinander vernetzt. Die einheitliche Fassade des Gebäudes ist durch vertikale Metallelemente filigran gegliedert. Zwischen und hinter den Lochblechelementen befinden sich Fenster, die sich für eine natürliche Belüftung öffnen lassen.

The individual storeys and departments are linked by a clear communication and circulation principle. Their interaction is encouraged by a winding staircase which acts as a meeting place and links each floor with the one above. The uniform façade of the building is divided into slender sections by vertical metal elements. Windows, some of which can be opened for natural ventilation, are located between and behind the perforated steel elements.

↖
Grundriss und Schnitt
Floor plan and section

Filmhaus des WDR
Generalsanierung

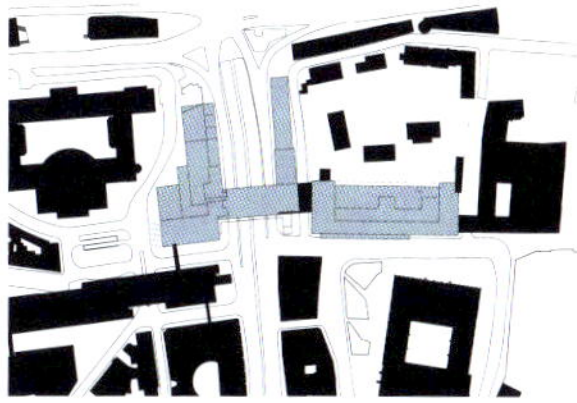

WDR Westdeutscher Rundfunk
Köln
2015

Technische Ausrüstung
IB Süss, München
Tragwerksplaner
Sailer Stepan und Partner, München
Bauphysik
Müller-BBM, Planegg

Wettbewerb 2015
Preisträger

Competition 2015
Award Winner

40 Jahre nach seiner Fertigstellung soll das Kölner Filmhaus des WDR am Appellhofplatz grundsaniert und zu einem modernen Medienhaus umgebaut werden. Insgesamt 40 Architekturbüros nahmen an dem eingeladenen internationalen Wettbewerb teil. Kommunikation und Vernetzung sind die zentralen Leitlinien des Entwurfs. Neben der energetischen Ertüchtigung des Gebäudes sieht das Umbaukonzept vor, herkömmliche Hierarchien und feste Nutzungscluster abzubauen und stattdessen ein Maximum an Flexibilität für heutige Arbeitsweisen zu ermöglichen. Die zehn Gebäudeebenen und ihre Flächen werden durch einen neuen Medienweg sowohl horizontal als auch vertikal miteinander verbunden. Wie ein Loop führt dieser Weg durch das gesamte Haus: er beginnt im Foyer, endet im WDR-Forum unter dem Dach und verleiht der crossmedialen Arbeitsweise der Rundfunkanstalt räumliche Gestalt. Am Schnittpunkt des Medienwegs mit den Brückenverbindungen zu den Nachbargebäuden des WDR liegt das neue interne Foyer, das mit einer Cafeteria zum Treffpunkt für alle Mitarbeiter wird. Die offene Treppe entlang

Forty years after its completion, the WDR Filmhaus Centre for Cinema Culture on Appellhofplatz in Cologne is to be completely refurbished and redesigned to create a modern media centre. Forty architectural offices took part in the invited international design competition. Communication and networking are the central themes of the design. In addition to the energy upgrade of the building, the redesign concept envisages the dissolution of conventional hierarchies and permanent usage clusters, and their replacement by maximum flexibility for modern ways of working. The ten levels of the building and their floors are connected horizontally and vertically by a new media thoroughfare. Like a loop, this thoroughfare leads the visitor through the whole building: beginning in the foyer and ending in the WDR Forum below the roof, it lends a spatial design element to the cross-media working environment of the broadcasting organisation. At the intersection of the media thoroughfare and the bridge connections to the neighbouring WDR buildings is a new internal foyer, which, along with its cafeteria,

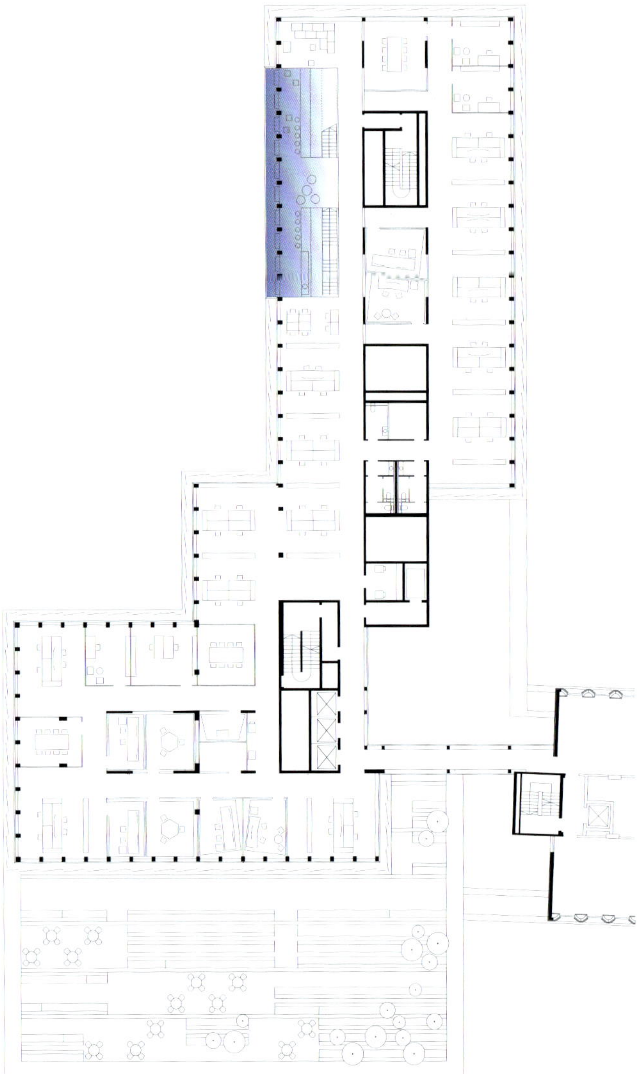

Grundriss 4. Obergeschoss
Floor plan 4th floor

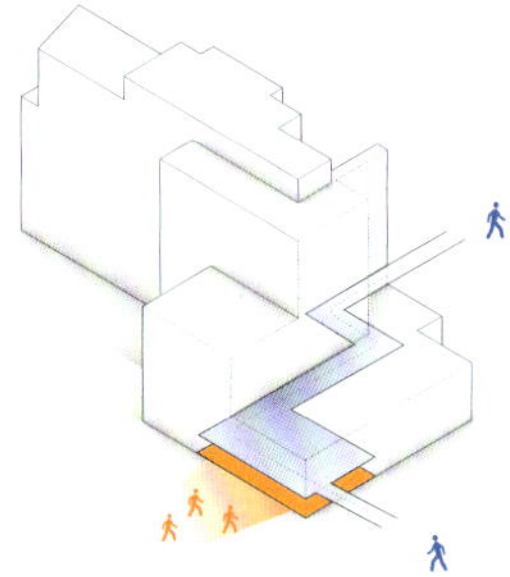

Zugang / Anschluss
Access / Connection

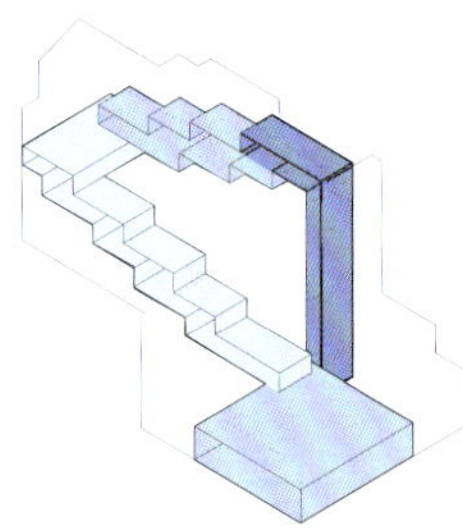

Loop

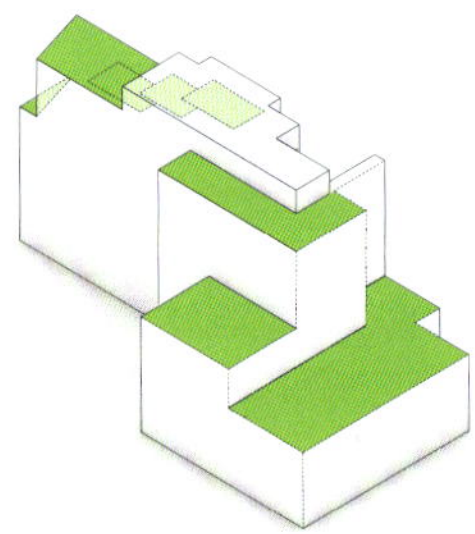

Dachflächen
Roof areas

der Fassade ist als Himmelsleiter konzipiert, sie ermöglicht kurze Wege zwischen den Etagen und bietet Raum für Kommunikation und informelle Begegnungen. Mit seinem neuen Haupteingang orientiert sich das Filmhaus zum Appellhofplatz, wo es Mitarbeiter und Besucher mit einer großzügigen architektonischen Geste willkommen heißt. Innen- und Außenraum, Vorplatz und Foyer gehen fließend ineinander über. Die neue Fassade ist mehrschichtig aufgebaut und hat eine äußere Schicht aus leicht verdrehten Prallscheiben. Neben ihrer energetischen Funktion geben die großflächigen Fassadenelemente dem gesamten Gebäude ein neues Gesicht. Die Festverglasung im Bereich des Loops macht die dynamische Innenwelt auch nach Außen hin sichtbar, sie stellt eine optische Verbindung zwischen den Innenräumen des Filmhauses und der Stadt dem Stadtraum her.

becomes the meeting point for all WDR staff. The open staircase along the façade is conceived as a "stairway to heaven", providing a short route between the floors and offering a space for communication and informal meetings. With its main entrance oriented towards Appellhofplatz, the Filmhaus welcomes employees and visitors with a generous architectural gesture. Interior and exterior spaces, forecourt and foyer flow into one another. The new façade is multi-layered; its outer skin being of slightly rotationally displaced protective baffle panels. In addition to their energy-related function, the large façade elements give the whole building a completely new appearance. The fixed glazing in the area of the loop makes the dynamic interior visible from the outside, creating an optical connection between the interior of the Filmhaus and its urban surroundings.

Himmelstreppe entlang der Fassade mit Ausblick auf Köln

Stairway along the façade with a view to the city of Cologne

Isar-Philharmonie

Ideenwettbewerb der NACHTSCHICHT 2015

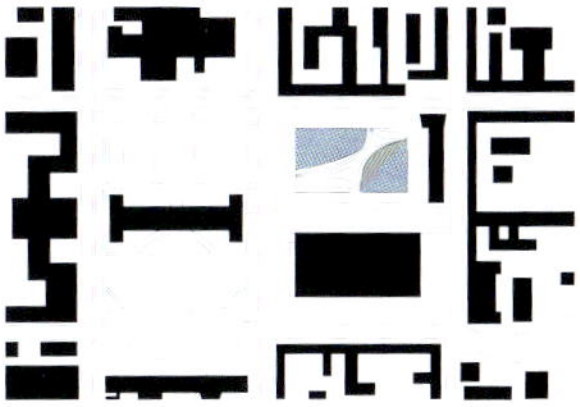

muenchenarchitektur.com
München
2015

Ideenwettbewerb 2015
Ideas Competition 2015

In der Debatte um den neuen Konzertsaal in München wurden mehrere Standortmöglichkeiten diskutiert.
Der Vorschlag für ein neues Konzerthaus an zentraler Stelle in der Maxvorstadt, gegenüber der Pinakothek der Moderne und am heutigen Standort der Geologischen Sammlung, geht vor allem von städtebaulichen Überlegungen aus. Das neue Gebäude für Münchens Orchester ergänzt das renommierte Kunstareal und stärkt seine Bedeutung als kulturelles Epizentrum der Stadt. War das Ensemble einzelner Museen bislang wenig zusammenhängend, so wird es durch den neuen Baustein des Konzerthauses miteinander vernetzt. Im Zusammenspiel mit den Pinakotheken entsteht ein Kulturareal, das auch außerhalb des Museumsbetriebs belebt ist.
Das Konzertgebäude nimmt die Proportionen der gegenüberliegenden Pinakothek der Moderne auf und lockert die strenge orthogonale Geometrie der Umgebung auf. Eine einladende, geschwungene Freitreppe gliedert das Grundstück diagonal in zwei Teile. Sie bildet einen belebten öffentlichen Raum, an dessen

Several possible development options were discussed in the debate about the new concert hall in Munich.
The proposal for a new concert hall in a central position in Maxvorstadt – opposite the Pinakothek der Moderne and on the present site of the Bavarian State Geological Collection, is based primarily on urban development considerations. The new building for Munich's orchestra enriches the famous Kunstareal (art district) and increases its importance as the cultural epicentre of the city. The ensemble of separate museums has been up until now somewhat disperate, however the new concert hall component will serve as an important interlocking point. Interaction with the Pinakothek will create an art district which will also energise the atmosphere in and around the museums.
The concert hall building takes up the proportions of the Pinakothek der Moderne opposite and the strict orthogonal geometry of its surroundings. An eases, invitingly open curved staircase divides the site diagonally into two parts, creating a vibrant open space with its

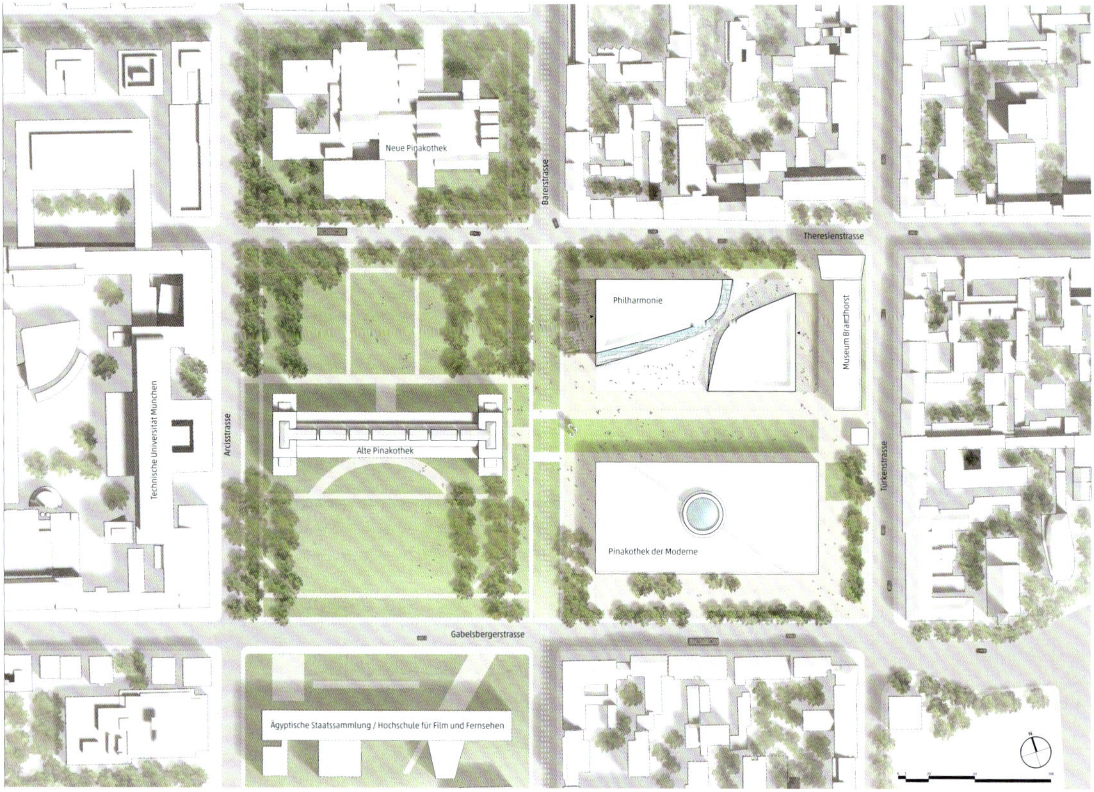
Neue Pinakothek
Barerstrasse
Theresienstrasse
Philharmonie
Museum Brandhorst
Technische Universität München
Arcisstrasse
Alte Pinakothek
Türkenstrasse
Pinakothek der Moderne
Gabelsbergerstrasse
Ägyptische Staatssammlung / Hochschule für Film und Fernsehen

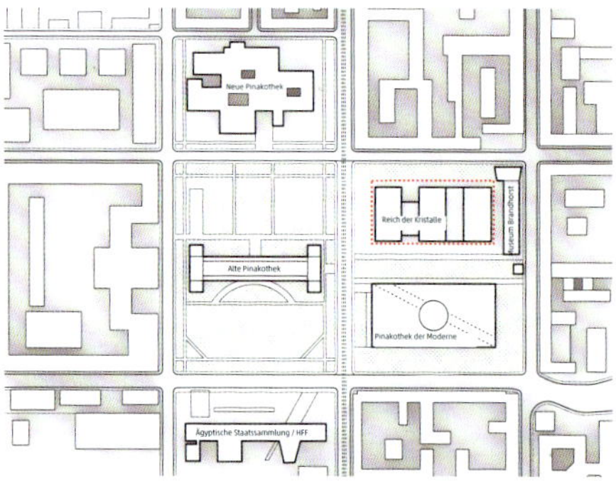
Neue Pinakothek
Reich der Kristalle
Museum Brandhorst
Alte Pinakothek
Pinakothek der Moderne
Ägyptische Staatssammlung / HFF

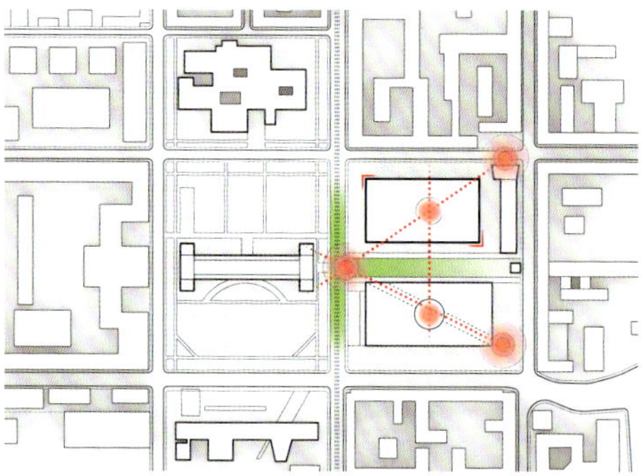

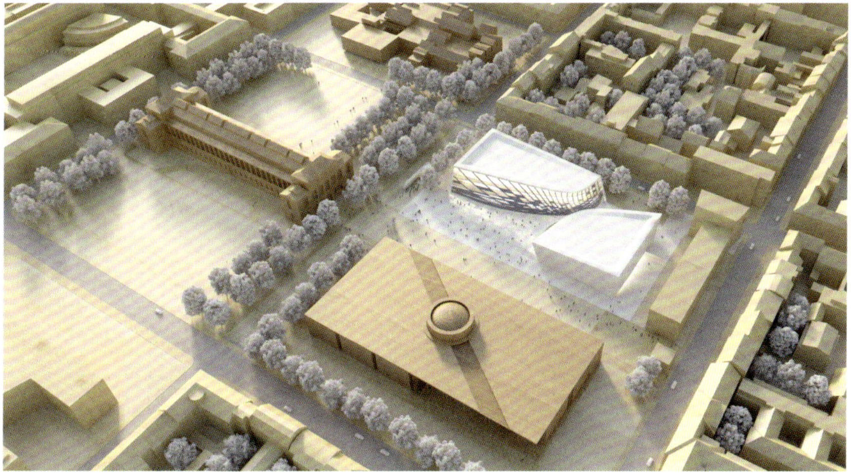

Scheitelpunkten die beiden seitlichen Konzertsäle erschlossen werden. Die Gebäude öffnen sich mit facettierten und gekrümmten Glasfassaden auf den öffentlichen Raum in ihrer Mitte. Ihre Architektur vernetzt die Pinakotheken und das gesamte Kunstareal mit dem angrenzenden Wohngebiet.

apex flanked by the two concert chambers. With their faceted and contorted glass façades, the buildings open up towards the public sphere in their midst. Their architecture links the Pinakothek and the entire Kunstareal area with the neighbouring residential district.

↖
Lageplan
Konzertsaal im Museumsareal in der Münchner Maxvorstadt

Site plan
Concert hall in the museum quarter of the Munich district Maxvorstadt

←←
Bestandssituation 2015
Existing site 2015

←
Achsen und Blickbeziehungen
Visual axes

Wettbewerbe 2015

South Technology University
Shenzhen, CN

Science Museum
Guangzhou, CN

Großmarkthalle
München

Nano Energy Institute
Beijing, CN

Neubau Nachhaltige Chemie
Straubing

Patton Barracks Masterplan
Heidelberg

Taiyuan Tower 2
Taiyuan, CN

Museum for Islamic Faith
Guangzhou, CN

TrappentreuTurm
München

Projekte weiterverfolgt

Groz-Beckert logistikhof
Albstadt

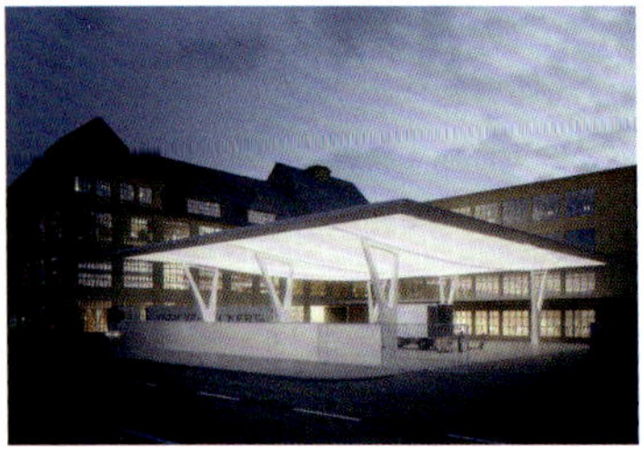

Groz-Beckert

Planung 2014
Bauzeit 2015
BGF 1.300 m²
Funktionen
Logistikhof
Status
Fertiggestellt

Carissma Forschungs- und Testzentrum
Ingolstadt

Staatliches Bauamt Ingolstadt

Planung 2012 - 2014
Bauzeit 2014 - 2016
BGF 5.600 m²
Funktion
Forschungs- und Testzentrum
für Fahrzeugsicherheit
Status
Bauphase

Philip Morris i-care
Crespellano, Italien

Philip Morris International

Planung 2013 - 2015
Bauzeit 2014 - 2016
BGF 75.000m²
Funktionen
Produktion, Logistik, Labore, Werkstätten, Verwaltung, Konferenzzentrum, Kantine, Umkleiden und Fitnessraum
Status
Bauphase

Arena 2036
Stuttgart

Baden-Württemberg

Planung 2014 - 2016
Bauzeit 2015 - 2016
BGF 9.884 m²
Funktion
Büro, Forschung und Entwicklung
Status
Bauphase

Paul-Klein-Zentrum für Immunintervention
Mainz

Universitätsmedizin Mainz

Planung	2012 - 2013 (BA 1)
	2014 - 2015 (BA 2)
	2014 - 2015 (BA 3)
Bauzeit	2013 - 2016 (BA 1)
	2016 - 2018 (BA 2)
	2016 - 2018 (BA 3)
BGF	9.370 m² (BA 1)
	13.348 m² (BA 2)
	3.856 m² (BA 3)

Funktionen
S2-Labore, Besprechungs-und Aufenthaltsbereiche, Büros (BA 1)
S2- und S3-Labore, Seminar- und Besprechungsbereich, Büros (BA 2)
MRT-Räume, Probandenuntersuchung, Büros, Besprechungs- und Seminarbereich (BA 3)
Status
Bauphase (BA 1), Planungsphase (BA 2+3)

Forschungszentrum Abbe Center of Photonics
Jena

Freistaat Thüringen Landesamt für Bau und Verkehr

Planung 2010 - 2013
Bauzeit 2013 - 2016
BGF 7.055 m²
Funktionen
Labore, Büros, Multimediaraum
Status
Bauphase

Technology Centre Knorr-Bremse Neubau TCK 3
München

Knorr-Bremse München

Planung 2013–2014
Bauzeit 2013–2016
BGF 16.900 m²
Funktionen
Forschungs- und Entwicklungsbereiche, Werkstatt, Büros, Showroom
Status
Bauphase

Technology Centre Knorr-Bremse Neubau TCK 2
München

Knorr-Bremse München

Planung 2015–2017
Bauzeit 2017–2019
BGF 31.000 m²
Funktionen
Forschungs- und Entwicklungsbereiche, Werkstatt, Büros, Showroom
Status
Konzeptphase

Proteinzentrum der Martin-Luther-Universität
Halle-Wittenberg

BLB Sachsen-Anhalt | Martin-Luther-Universität

Planung 2013 - 2015
Bauzeit 2014 - 2016
BGF 10.300 m²
Funktionen
S1- und S2-Labore, Büro-, Seminar-, Aufenthalts- und Besprechungsräume
Status
Bauphase

BMW FIZ Sanierung Eingangsgebäude
München

BMW Group

Planung 2014 - 2015
Bauzeit 2013 - 2016
BGF 19.500 m²
Funktionen
Zentraleingang, Besprechungszone, Teambüros, Vorstandsbüros, Casino, Caféteria, Teeküchen
Status
Bauphase

Siemens Sektor Healthcare
Forchheim

Siemens AG

Planung 2011 - 2013
Bauzeit 2013 - 2016
BGF 43.850 m²
Funktionen
Büros, Werkstätten, Kantine, Schulungs- und Konferenzzentrum, Rechenzentrum
Status
Bauphase

Faculté Necker, Université Descartes Paris
Paris, Frankreich

Université René Descartes

Planung 2011 - 2014
Bauzeit 2014 - 2017
BGF 22.500 m²
Funktionen
Labore, Caféteria, Hörsäle, Seminarräume, Bibliothek
Status
Bauphase

VW Windkanal - Effizienzzentrum
Wolfsburg

Volkswagen AG

Planung 2012 - 2016
Bauzeit 2015 - 2016
BGF 16.800 m²
Funktionen
Prüfstände, Werkstätten, Büros
Status
Bauphase

Bau für Geisteswissenschaften
Bochum

Ruhr-Universität Bochum | BLB NRW

Planung 2011 - 2013
Bauzeit 2014 - 2018
BGF 39.200 m²
Funktion
Wissenschaftliche Institute, Seminar- und Verwaltungsräume, Hörsäle, Bibliothek, Caféteria
Status
Bauphase

RWTH Aachen / Campus Melaten / Cluster Produktionstechnik
Aachen

Immofinanz Group, Wien

Planung 2014 - 2015
Bauzeit 2015 - 2016
BGF 33.000 m² (BA1)
Funktionen
Büros-, Entwicklungs- und Forschungseinrichtungen, Dienstleitung, Caféteria
Status
Planungsphase, Bauphase

KFW Büro – und Schulungszentrum
Frankfurt / Main

KFW Bankengruppe

Planung 2013 - 2014
Bauzeit 2013 - 2016
BGF 10.640 m²
Funktionen
Büros, Caféteria, Schulungs- und Konferenzräume, Tiefgarage
Status
Bauphase

MTU Werkserweiterung
Rzeszów, Polen

MTU Aero Engines Polska

Planung 2013
Bauzeit 2013 - 2015
BGF 10.470 m²
Funktionen
Produktion, Datenzentrum, Büros, Administration
Status
Fertiggestellt

China Life Training Centre
Chengdu, China

China Life

Planung 2010 - 2011
Bauzeit 2012 - 2014
BGF 102.000 m²
Funktionen
Schulung, Konferenz, Hotel, Archiv, Gastronomie
Status
Fertiggestellt

Hyundai Motor Company Design Centre
Seoul, Korea

Hyundai Motor Company

Planung Phase1 2013
Bauzeit Phase 1 2014 - 2015
Planung Phase 2 2015
Planung Phase 2 2016 - 2017
BGF 30 000 m²
Funktionen
Büros, Werkstatt, Entwicklungszentrum
Status
Bauphase

Huanglong International Centre
Hangzhou, China

Canhigh Construction Group

Planung 2014 - 2015
Bauzeit 2015 - 2017
BGF 106.348 m²
Funktionen
Büros, Commercial
Status
Design Development

BMW Brilliance Automotive R&D-Centre-
Shenyang, China

BMW Brilliance Automotive

Planung 2013 - 2015
Bauzeit 2015 - 2016
BGF 38.664 m²
Funktionen
Büro, Kantine, Prüfstand, Werkstatt Prototypen
Status
Bauphase

China Life Research & Development Centre
Peking, China

China Life

Planung 2008 - 2011
Bauzeit 2011 - 2016
BGF 398.000 m²
Funktionen
Innovationszentrum, Rechenzentrum, Schulungsgebäude, Mitarbeiterrestaurant, Apartmenthaus für Mitarbeiter, Sportanlagen
Status
Bauphase

Recife Research & Development Centre
Recife, Brasilien

Fiat Chrysler Automobiles

Planung 2015
BGF 25.000 m²
Funktionen
Masterplan, R&D Gebäude, Büros, Prüfstand

HENN PROZESSE

Innovation durch Kooperation
PROGRAMMING, PERFORMING und APPROVING stärken als Querschnittsfunktionen unsere Projekte. Durch kontinuierliche Beratung und Recherche begleiten sie das Design, die Planung und die Realisierung.
Während PROGRAMMING im Dialog mit den Bauherren schon vor dem Entwurfsstadium Klarheit über den Kontext von Projekten schafft und Ziele definiert, greift PERFORMING in der Planungsphase. Durch die Recherche zu Materialien und Energiefragen stellen wir sicher, dass neueste Entwicklungen und Forschungsergebnisse im Bereich der Smart Materials, der Bausysteme oder der Energietechnologien in die Planung integriert werden. APPROVING setzt in der Realisierungsphase ein, es kontrolliert und prüft die Umsetzbarkeit mit Bezug auf vorhandene Richtlinien und Normen. Gemeinsam wirken die drei Instrumente auf unsere internen Prozesse und fördern dadurch die Qualität und Besonderheit unserer Bauten.

Innovation through cooperation
PROGRAMMING, PERFORMING and APPROVING are cross-divisional functions which strengthen our projects and accompany the design, planning and realisation processes by means of consultancy and research.
While PROGRAMMING creates clarity with regard to project context and defines targets in dialogue with the client even before the design stage, PERFORMING takes effect in the planning phase. By studying materials and energy matters, we ensure that the latest developments and research findings in the fields of smart materials, construction systems and energy technologies are integrated in planning. APPROVING is deployed in the realisation phase; it monitors and checks the feasibility in relation to existing directives and standards. The three instruments work together on our internal processes, thereby promoting the quality and uniqueness of our architecture.

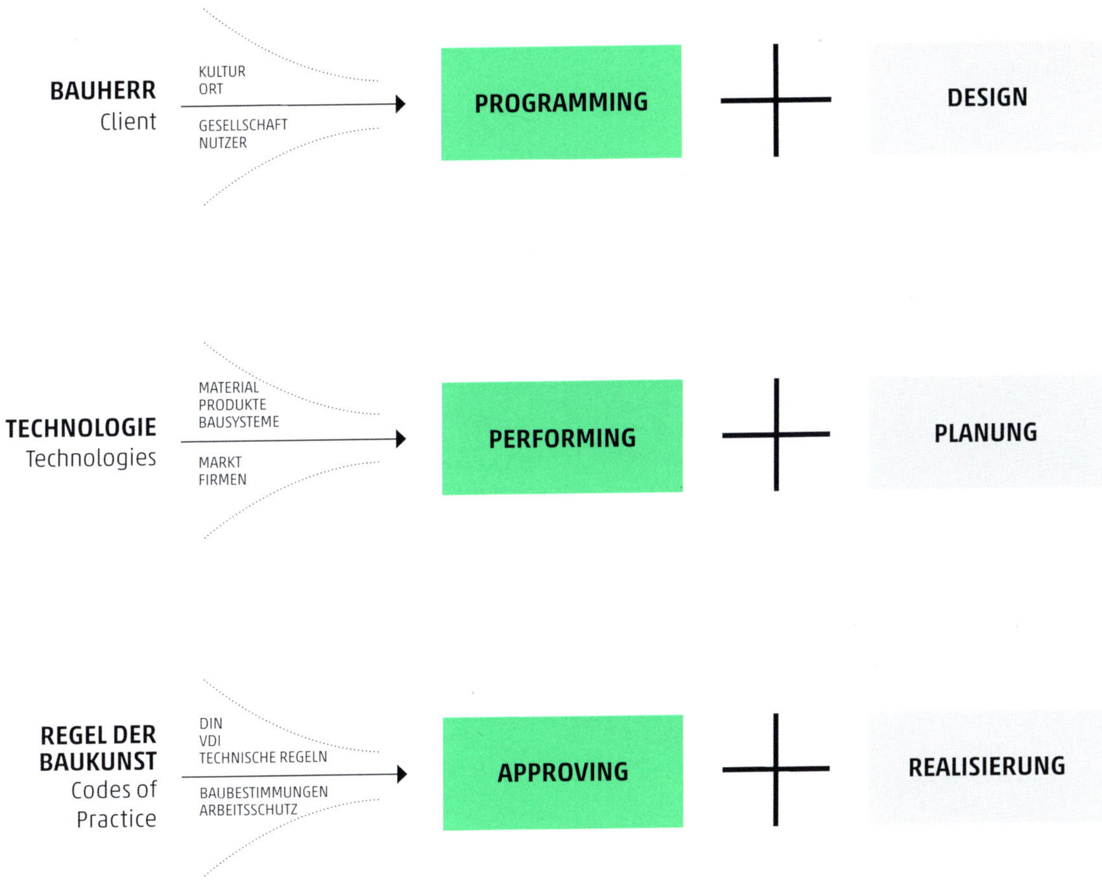
BAUHERR
Client
KULTUR
ORT
GESELLSCHAFT
NUTZER
PROGRAMMING
DESIGN
TECHNOLOGIE
Technologies
MATERIAL
PRODUKTE
BAUSYSTEME
MARKT
FIRMEN
PERFORMING
PLANUNG
REGEL DER BAUKUNST
Codes of Practice
DIN
VDI
TECHNISCHE REGELN
BAUBESTIMMUNGEN
ARBEITSSCHUTZ
APPROVING
REALISIERUNG

PROGRAMMING

Konzept braucht Kontext
Mit PROGRAMMING verwenden wir eine Denk- und Arbeitsweise, die sich auf den ganzheitlichen Kontext des Projektes konzentriert und ihn sichtbar macht. Jedes PROGRAMMING startet mit einem intensiven Dialog beim Bauherren vor Ort. Gemeinsam diskutieren wir die wesentlichen Themen, wägen ihre Relevanz ab und strukturieren die Ergebnisse. Ziel dabei ist es, Prozesse wie den der Innovation in das Medium des Raumes zu übersetzen. Der Bauherr erhält so die Sicherheit, frühzeitig die richtigen Entscheidungen zu treffen und quantitative sowie qualitative Anforderungen genau zu definieren. Dieses Verfahren gibt uns die Möglicheit, räumliche Unterscheidungen zu treffen und deren Interaktion festzulegen. Elementar ist insgesamt, die Einzigartigkeit jedes Projekts herauszukristallisieren und Themenschwerpunkte zu setzen. Die Form des Gebäudes muss sich dann am Kontext messen lassen, damit ganzheitliche Konzepte und gelungene Architektur entstehen.

Concept needs context
With PROGRAMMING, we use a mind-set and method of working that concentrates on the holistic context of the project and makes it visible. Each PROGRAMMING process begins with an intensive dialogue with the client on site. We discuss together the essential themes, weigh up their relevance and structure the results with the aim of translating processes, such as innovation, into the medium of architecture. In this way the client can be assured of taking the right decisions in good time and is enabled to precisely define quantitative and qualitative requirements. The procedure provides us, as architects, with the necessary opportunity to make spatial distinctions and to determine their interaction. It is of fundamental importance on the whole to emphasise the unique nature of the project and to focus on radical key themes. The shape of the building must be measured in context so that comprehensive concepts and successful architecture can come into being.

Platz
Central plaza

Magistrale
Central axis

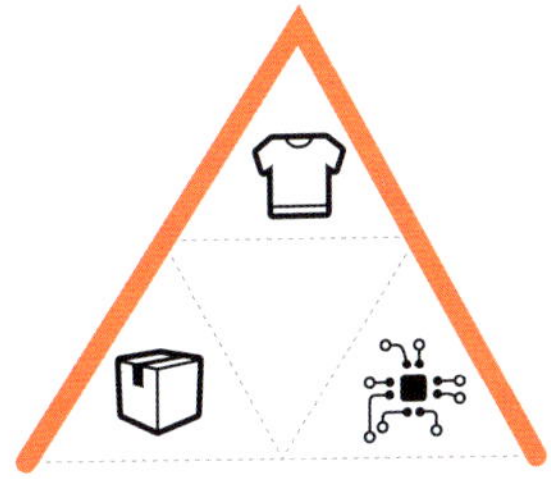

Dach
Roof

Öffnen
Open

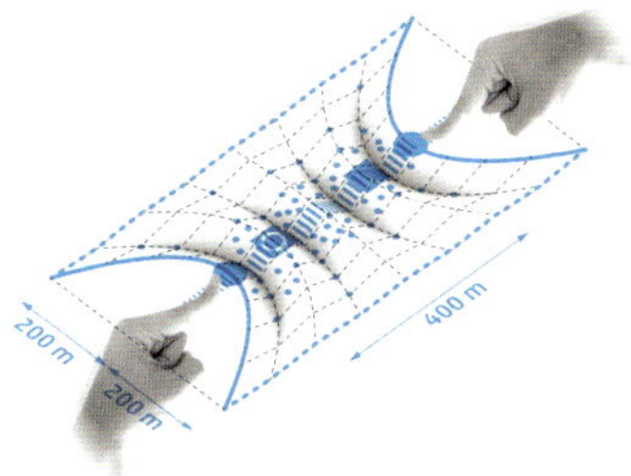

Verkürzen
Contract

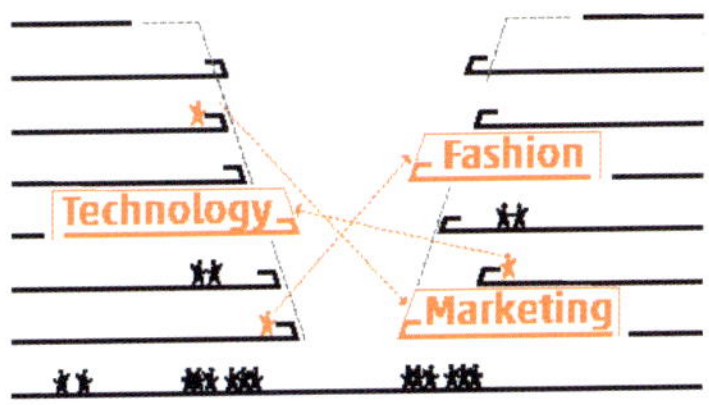

Vernetzen
Interconnect

Emanuel-Merck-Platz, Darmstadt

BMW FIZ Future, München

Zalando Headquarters, Berlin

PERFORMING

Architektur braucht Research

Das Performance Based Design (PERFORMING) bündelt unsere interne Recherche und Beratung zum Entwurfs- und Planungsprozess von Projekten. Ziel des PERFORMING ist ein objektives Feedback zu Fragen des Materials und der Energie. Der angemessene Einsatz von Materialien und ihre Kombination sind entscheidend für die Identität, die Wirkung und die Langlebigkeit von Gebäuden. Deshalb wägen wir den Einsatz von Hightech und Lowtech sowie traditionelle und innovative Materiallösungen in einem rationalen Auswahlverfahren ab. Die Energieberatung zu einzelnen Gebäuden berücksichtigt auch vorhandene lokale Ressourcen. Sonne, Wind und der klimatische Kontext werden in die Konzeption und die Detailplanung von Fassadensystemen einbezogen. Die präzise Reaktion der Architektur auf diese Parameter ist maßgeblich, weil sie die Interaktion zwischen dem Gebäude und seiner Umgebung bestimmen.

Architecture needs research

Performance-based design (PERFORMING) bundles our internal research and consultancy activities into the design and planning process of projects. The aim of PERFORMING is to generate objective feedback with regard to materials and energy. The appropriate deployment of materials and their combination are decisive for the identity, impact and permanence of buildings. We therefore weigh up the use of high-tech and low-tech as well as traditional and innovative material solutions in a rational selection process. Energy consultancy for individual buildings takes into account local resources. Sun, wind and the climatic context are taken into consideration at the conception and detailed planning stages of facade systems. The precise reaction of architecture to these parameters is decisive because this determines the interaction between the building and its surroundings.

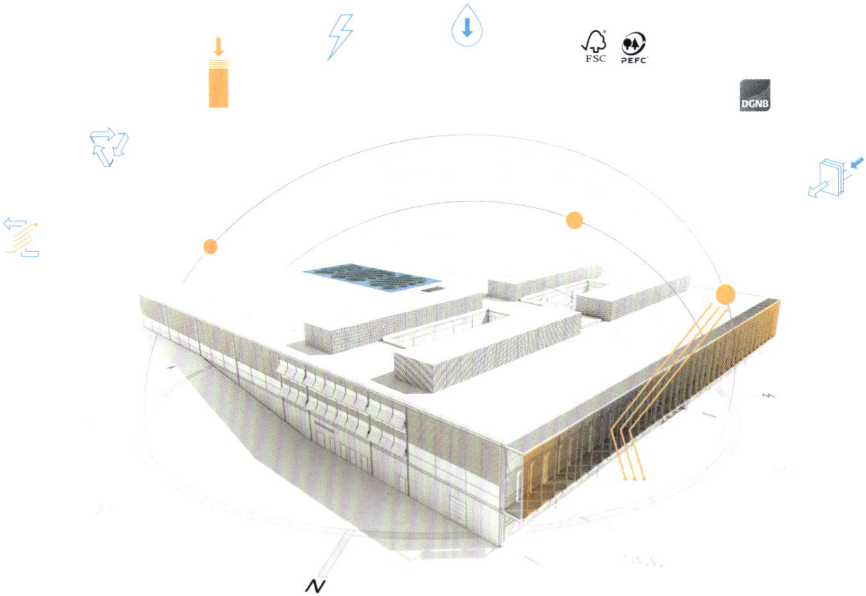

Nachhaltigkeitsdiagramm
Sustainability diagram

APPROVING

Qualität braucht Kontrolle
Zur erfolgreichen Entwicklung von Bauvorhaben ist Qualitätsmanagement unabdingbar. Deshalb greift unser internes APPROVING auf verschiedenen Ebenen. Wir messen die Leistungsfähigkeit von Projekten hinsichtlich vordefinierter Ziele und stellen so ihre Qualität sicher. In Meetings werden die Ziele einzelner Leistungsphasen klar definiert. Mithilfe von Checklisten überprüfen wir die Vor- und Entwurfsplanungen. Die interne Kontrolle greift besonders tief bei der Vollständigkeit und der Richtigkeit aller Gewerkplanungen und -ausschreibungen. Zur Fortbildung unserer Mitarbeiter führen wir regelmäßig interne Seminare durch. Bei Sonderkonstruktionen und innovativen Bauarten steht die Aufklärung und Risikobewertung in unserem Fokus. Zentrale Bedeutung für das Qualitätsmanagement hat außerdem die Standardisierung und Pflege ausgewählter Arbeitsmittel.

Quality needs control
Quality management is indispensable for the successful development of construction projects. Therefore our internal APPROVING process operates at different levels. We measure the performance capability of projects with regard to pre-defined targets and in this way ensure their quality. The targets of individual performance phases are clearly defined in meetings. With the help of checklists we examine preliminary plans and the conceptual design. The internal control mechanisms are particularly meticulous with regard to the completeness and correctness of all planning and tendering procedures. We hold regular internal seminars for the further training of our employees. In the case of special constructions and innovative designs, we focus on clarification and risk assessment. Standardisation and maintenance of selected working materials are of central importance for quality management.

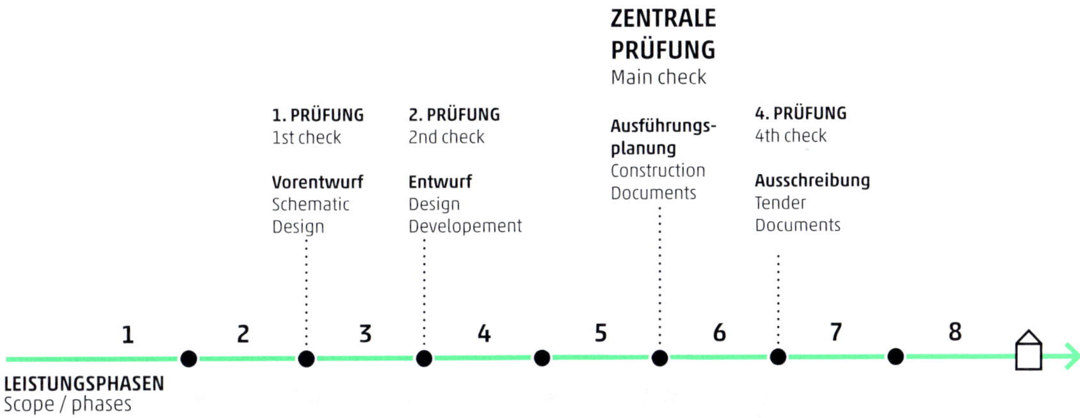

Interne Fortbildung
Internal Training

KickOff und Prüfung
Kickoff and verification

Freigabe
Approval

Interne Weiterbildungen 2015

HENN Büro München / Büro Berlin

Fr 30.01.15 / Fr 06.02.15
Martin Erdinger: Neue Normen und Regelwerke aus 2014

Fr 06.03.15 / Fr 20.03.15
Jan Leo Archut: Brandschutz – Was Zulassungen zulassen und was Bauprodukte nicht können

Fr 27.03.15 / Fr 10.04.15
Thomas von Küstenfeld: HENN CAD Standard – Vorteile und Nutzen für die CAD-Planung

Fr 24.04.15 / Fr 08.05.15
Martin Erdinger: Grundlagen des Brandschutzes, Inhalte eines Brandschutznachweises

Fr 26.06.15 / Fr 03.07.15
Sonja Millauer: Rechtssicherer und vertragsrelevanter Schriftverkehr, wenn die Schieflage droht

Fr 17.07.15 / Fr 10.07.15
Martin Erdinger: Schallschutz

Fr 24.07.15 / Fr 17.07.15
Thomas von Küstenfeld: Projektstartprozess - CAD Projektbegleitung durch Design Systems

Fr 11.09.15 / Fr 04.09.15
Firma Zeidler & Wimmel, Enrico Kops: Naturstein – Gesteinskunde / Klassifizierung / Anwendung / Nachweise

Fr 18.09.15 / Fr 25.09.15
Falk Flade: Baustelleneinrichtung, Baulogistik und Feinstaubminderung

Fr 02.10.15 / Fr 13.11.15
Manfred Sauer: Systemvergleich – Einzelvergabe / Funktional / GU, worauf es ankommt

Fr 09.10.15 / Fr 23.10.15
Wolfgang Wrba: VOB – Die wichtigsten Paragraphen

Fr 30.10.15 / Fr 06.11.15
Axel Mierisch: Sichtbeton – Handwerkskunst der Einfachheit

Fr 13.11.15 / Fr 20.11.15
Thomas von Küstenfeld: BIM @ HENN – Status Quo und die Zukunft

Fr 20.11.15 / Fr 13.11.15
Thomas Margaretha: Spezialtiefbau – Wie eine komplexe Baugrube entsteht und vergeht

Vorträge HENN 2015

Gunter Henn

22. Januar // Forum Architektur, Messe München
„BMW FIZ Future –
Masterplan BMW Forschungs-und Innovationszentrum 2050, München"

14. März // Bayerische Staatskanzlei, Landshut
„Identität und Architektur"

17. März // Labor-Impuls Forum, Berlin
„Bauten für die Wissenschaft"

24. April // AGI Frühjahrstagung, Turku, Finnland
„Embodyment of Innovation – Dynamic spaces"

06. / 07. Mai // Fachhändlertagung, Weil am Rhein
„Embodyment of Innovation – Dynamic spaces"

27. Mai // Technologiezentren, Adlershof
„Architektur für Forschung, Entwicklung und Produktion"

18. Juni // Leichtbausymposium, Dresden
„Die Leichtigkeit des Designs"

11. September // merTens AG, Willich
„Die Entwicklung der Arbeitswelten"

24. September // Zentrum für Photovoltaik, Adlershof
„Kommunikation und Konzentration"

29. September // Aachen
Exzellente Fabriken planen + bauen
„Factory of the Future: Empowering for Industry 4.0"

04. November // TU, Budapest, Ungarn
„Thinking Architecture"

06. November // International PhD Program –
Graduation Day, Dresden
„Architecture of Distinction"

Martin Henn

02. Oktober // Harvard Design, Chicago, USA
Adaptive Architectures and Smart Materials Conference
„Transparencies"

Norbert Schachtner

26. Juni // "Die Klinikimmobilie der nächsten Generation", Frankfurt
„Arbeitswelten für die Wissenschaft"

WITTENSTEIN Innovationsfabrik, Harthausen

Zentrum für Photovoltaik, Berlin

Hypo Vereinsbank Filiale, München

Nestlé Kaffeefabrik, Schwerin

HVB-Tower, München

Merck Innovationszentrum, Darmstadt

Siemens Healthcare, Forchheim

Nachhaltigkeitszertifizierungen

DGNB Platin

DGNB Gold

Nachhaltigkeitskriterien werden bei HENN über den gesamten Projektablauf berücksichtigt. Möchten Bauherren die verschiedenen Nachhaltigkeitskriterien im Projekt mit einem Zertifikat abschließen, so wird der Zertifizierungsprozess von eigenen Auditoren- und Beratungsteam betreut, das in engem Kontakt mit der Zertifizierungsstelle der Deutschen Gesellschaft für Nachhaltiges Bauen und dem U.S. Green Building Council steht. Wir berücksichtigen das gewünschte Zertifizierungsziel bei sämtlichen Maßnahmen der Projektarbeit. Dabei werden besondere Themenfelder wie die Bedingungen am Arbeitsplatz oder die Einbindung aller verbauten Materialien in einen geschlossenen Materialkreislauf ausformuliert. Im Jahr 2015 wurden die beiden ersten durch federführende Auditoren zertifizierten Bauvorhaben ausgezeichnet - die WITTENSTEIN Innovationsfabrik mit DGNB Platin sowie die Nestlé Kaffeefabrik mit LEED Gold. Weitere Zertifizierungen für das Merck Innovation Centre, den HVB-Tower oder dem Siemens Healthcare Gebäude werden aktuell bearbeitet.

Sustainability criteria are taken into consideration by HENN during the entire course of the project. If clients wish to obtain certification with regard to the various sustainability criteria in the project, this process will be accompanied by an auditing and consultancy team in close cooperation with the certification body of the German Sustainable Building Council (DNGB) and the U.S. Green Building Council. We take into account the desired certification objective with all measures connected with project work, while formulating special thematic fields, such as workplace conditions or the integration of all building materials in a closed material cycle. In 2015, the first two certified construction projects obtained awards from leading auditors: the WITTENSTEIN Innovation Factory was awarded with DGNB Platinum and the Nestlé Coffee Factory with LEED Gold. Further certifications for the Merck Innovation Centre, the HVB Tower and the Siemens Healthcare Building are currently under review.

Masterplan St. Catherine Senior High School for Girls, Agbakope

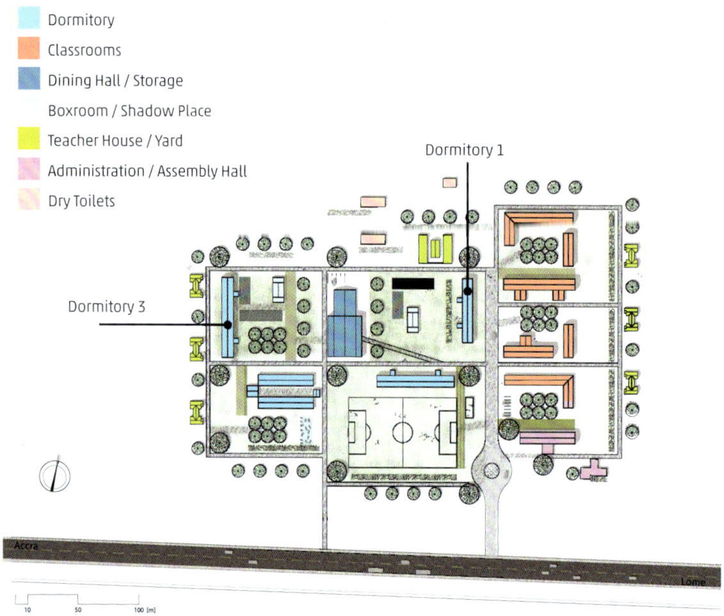

Dormitory 1 (2011)

Dormitory 3 – part I (2015)

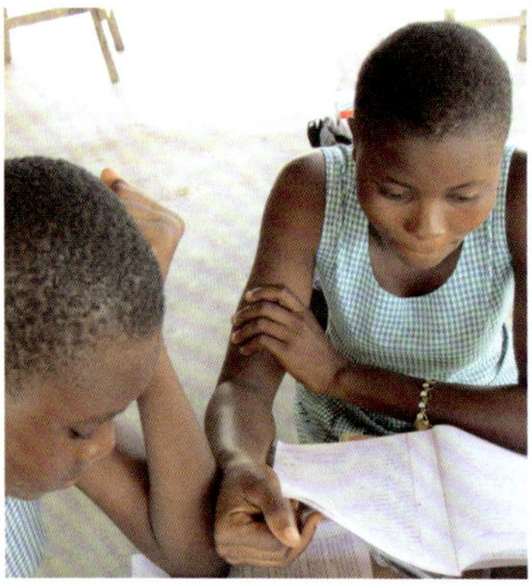

Dormitory 3 – part II (2016)

AddYouCation. Schule für alle Kinder.

AddYouCation. School for all children.

AddYouCation e.V.
München
gegründet 2009
www.addyoucation.com

AddYouCation ist ein gemeinnütziger Verein mit dem Ziel, Schulprojekte in Regionen zu fördern, wo sie besonders dringend gebraucht werden und die Realisierung durch professionellen Einsatz direkt vor Ort zu gewährleisten. Seit 2009 hat AddYouCation eine aktive Rolle beim Bau der St. Catherine Senior High School in Ghana übernommen – ein Projekt, das als einzige weiterführende und verantwortungsvoll geleitete Mädchenschule in der Region bereits sehr anerkannt ist. Damit der Campus dieser Internatsschule auch in Zukunft wachsen kann, setzt sich AddYouCation für die Errichtung weiterer Gebäude und die Betreuung von Patenschaften ein. Nach der Finanzierung und dem Bau des ersten, 2011 fertiggestellten Dormitorys, konnte 2014 auch ein Großteil des dritten Dormitorys durch AddYouCation finanziert werden. Ein weiterer Spendenbetrag wird die komplette Fertigstellung des Gebäudes sicherstellen, damit alle der derzeit 580 Schülerinnen auf dem Campus wohnen können.
AddYouCation wird unterstützt von Mitgliedern, Paten und Spendern.

AddYouCation is a charity initiative dedicated to supporting school projects in regions where they are needed most and to guarantee the realisation of projects through the provision of professional support on site.
In 2009 AddYouCation took an active role in helping to build the St. Catherine Senior High School in Ghana. The initiative is now well known for this project. It is the only secondary school for girls which is responsibly managed in this region. AddYouCation is committed to realising additional building structures on campus as well as supporting sponsorships in order to enable the future development of the boarding school. In 2011 the construction of the first dormitory on site was financed and supervised by AddYouCation. A great part of the construction of the third dormitory was financed by AddYouCation in 2014, the building will now be completed with a final donation, so that 580 current students can live on the school campus.

AddYouCation's efforts are supported by members, sponsors and donors.

Spendenkonto
Donation account
AddYouCation e.V.
HypoVereinsbank AG München
IBAN
DE81700202700066074501
BIC
HYVEDEMMXXX

Veröffentlichungen 2015

Attocube Systems, München

Nano-Manufaktur am Haarer Dreieck
Bernhard Lohr
in: Süddeutsche Zeitung, Ausgabe Landkreis Müchen Nord, 30.07.2015, S. R9

Carissma, Ingolstadt

Carissma
in: Forschungsbericht TH Ingolstadt 2015, 1 2015, S. 16-22

Carissma: vom Spatenstich zu Richtfest
in: Thimotion, TH Ingolstadt, 2 2015, S. 31-33

DRX

Call for Application DRX 2015
in: www.dezeen.com, 10.04.2015

Gläserne Manufaktur, Dresden

Arbeiten und Wohlfühlen
Gerhard Matzig
in: Süddeutsche Zeitung, 20.01.2015, S.19

Henn allgemein + Programming

Wissensmanagement beflügelt
in: Buch, Beier, Heiko; Schmidt, Ulrich; Klett, Davis (HRSG)
Nagel, André, Steinbusch, Michael, Gunter HENN, u.a.
Akademische Verlagsgesellschaft AKA GmbH, Berlin, 2015

Wettbewerb(ung) sonnvoll oder sinnlos?
Tim Bauerfeind
in: Der Entwurf - Supplement der DBZ , April 2015, S.15

HVB-Tower, München

Modernisierung des HVB-Tower - Moderne trifft Tradition
in: Wirtschaft + Architektur

Bauelite trifft Deutschland 2015
in: IMMOSALE UG 2015, S. 208-209

Innovationsfabrik Wittenstein, Igersheim-Harthausen

Entwicklungs- und Produktionsgebäude für Antriebssysteme in Igersheim
Emilia Margaretha
in: Detail, Detail Verlag, Nr. 3 2015, S. 190 - 192

Wittenstein Innovationsfabrik in Igersheim
in: www.baunetzwissen.de, 28.07.2015

Präzise Durchlass-Technik
Heribert Monitz
in: bba 10 2015, S. 64-66

Die Wittenstein Innovationsfabrik: ausgezeichnet für nachhaltiges Bauen
in: Pressebox, Wittenstein AG, 09.11.2015

Inselspital Bern

Städtebau für Spitzenmedizin
in: TEC21, sia, No. 38, 2015, S. 17

Max-Planck-Institut für Hirnforschung, Frankfurt am Main

Max-Planck-Institut für Hirnforschung, Frankfurt am Main
in: Stein Objekte 02, 2015, S. 166-167

Merck Innovationszentrum, Darmstadt

Kleeblatt mit Rampen
in: www.baunetz.de, 09.11.2015

Liquid crystal windows im Innovationszentrum von Merck
in: Displaying Futures, Merck, 1 2015, S. 14-15

Porsche Pavillon Wolfsburg

Porsche Pavilion in der Autostadt in Wolfsburg, HENN, München I Finalisten
in: Stahl Innovationspreis 2015, S. 26

Proteinzentrum Halle

Ein Ort der Spitzenforschung
Julius Lukas
in: Mitteldeutsche Zeitung, 18.12.2014

Robert-Koch-Instutut, Haus 6, Berlin

Killerviren in Wedding
Kathrin Zinkant
in: Süddeutsche Zeitung, 10.02.2015

Berlin: Merkel eröffnet neues Hochsicherheitslabor des Robert-Koch-Instituts
in: www.tagesschau.de
Video, 03.02.2015 20:18 Uhr

Eröffnung des neuen Laborgebäudes des Robert-Koch-Instituts mit Rede von Bundeskanzlerin Angela Merkel am 03.02.2015
in: www.youtube.de

Wettbewerbe

Sanierung des WDR Filmhauses: Architektenentwürfe gehen in die nächste Runde
in: www.presseportal.de, 01.05.2015

Arena 2036
in: exact Kundenmagazin, 7 2015, S. 10

Völlig losgelöst
Evelyn Vogel
in: Süddeutsche Zeitung, 14.07.2015, S. R18

Wissenswerkstatt Gmünder Eule, Schwäbisch Gmünd

Die „Eule" zum Fressen gern
Anja Jantschuk
in: Gmünder Tagespost, 10.05.2015

Zalando Headquarter, Berlin

Ein Raumschiff in Friedrichshain
in: Süddeutsche Zeitung, 20.11.2015, S. 23

HENN to design new Zalando HQ in Berlin
in: www.bustler.net, 20.11.2015

HENN Architects Wins Competition to Design New Zalando Headquarters in Berlin
in: www.archdaily.com, 21.11.2015

HENN gewinnt 1. Preis für Zalando Hauptsitz in Berlin
in: www.detail.de, 17.11.2015

HENN baut für Zalando
in: industriebau-online.de, 19.11.2015

Zalando baut neue Bürogebäude in Friedrichshain
in: www.morgenpost.de, 17.11.2015

Catwalks und Neighbourhoods
in: www.baunetz.de, 17.11.2015

An der Spree entsteht der größte Schuhkarton der Stadt
Friederike Corts
in: Bild Zeitung Berlin, 17.11.2015, S. 13

Auf dem Weg zur Denkfabrik
Jochen Knoblach
in: Berliner Zeitung, 17.11.2015

Zalando baut neuen Campus in Berlin Friedrichshain
in: www.berliner-zeitung.de, 17.11.2015

Zalando breitet sich am Ostbahnhof aus
in: www.immobilienmanager.de, 17.11.2015

Friedrichshain wird Zalando-Stadt
Maris Hubschmid
in: Tagespiegel, 17.11.2015

HENN Zalando Hauptsitz
in: www.german-architects.com, 17.11.2015

Berlin: Weitere 42.000 m^2 Bürofläche für Zalando
in: www.thomas-daily.de, 17.11.2015

Zalando baut neue Firmenzentrale für 140 Millionen Euro
in: www.gruenderszene.de, 17.11.2015

Zalando baut neuen Campus für 140 Millionen Euro
in: www.silicon.de, 17.11.2015

Zalando bekommt 2018 einen neuen Büro-Campus in Berlin
in: www.haufe.de, 17.11.2015

Zalando constuirá un campus de oficinas en Berlín con capacidad para 5.000 empleados
in: www.europapress.es, 17.11.2015

Zalando expandiert in Berlin
in: www.immobilienzeitung.de, 17.11.2015

HENN wins 1st prize for Zalando's Headquarters in Berlin
in: www.e-architect.co.uk, 17.11.2015

Zalando-Campus wird in Berlin entwickelt
in: www.konii.de, 17.11.2015

Zalando: Ein Campus wie im Valley, nur halt in Berlin
in: www.fabeau.de, 17.11.2015

Zalando plant in Berlin ein riesiges Büro-Ufo für 5000 Mitarbeiter
in: www.wired.de, 17.11.2015

Zalando-Campus: 2000 neue Jobs an modernen Arbeitsplätzen
in: www.berlinonline.de, 17.11.2015

Zalando-Campus wird auf dem Anschutz-Areal in Berlin entwickelt
in: www.deal-magazin.com, 17.11.2015

Zalando Builds Huge 100,000 Square Metre Office in Berlin
in: www.ecomony.com, 17.11.2015

Zentrum für Photovoltaik, Berlin-Adlershof

Maßgeschneidert
in: bba bau beratung architektur, 5 2015, S. 26-27

Impressum

HENN

Geschäftsführung Gunter Henn
Partner Christian Bechtle, Marcus Fissan, Martin Henn, Frank Hoffmeister,
Paul Lawrence, Axel Mathony, Georg Pichler, Norbert Schachtner,
Stefan Sinning, Rainer Sladek, Werner Sonnleitner, Wolfgang Wrba
Partner China Matthias Lassen, Wei Sun

Redaktion HENN Communications Team
Texte Sandra Hofmeister, Michael Steinbusch
Übersetzungen STS Schellnack Translation Service

Druck Steininger Offsetdruck

Bereits erschienen
Jahrbücher 2002, 2003, 2004, 2005, 2006, 2007, 2008, 2009, 2010, 2011, 2012/13, 2013/14, 2015
Aedes Die Autostadt (2000), Architektur des Wissens (2003),
Gläserne Manufaktur (2003), Das Projekthaus (2004), Bugatti Molsheim (2005),
Henn 30/30 (2010), MobileLifeCampus (2011),
Max Planck Institute for Brain Research Frankfurt (2014)
WITTENSTEIN Innovationsfabrik (2016)

Abbildungen
Modelle, Renderings, Zeichnungen, Fotos: HENN
WITTENSTEIN/Joachim Schmeisser: S. 154
diephotodesigner.de: S. 96 – 101
Su Zhe Wei: S. 66, 141 – 143
Heinz von Heydenaber: S. 151
HG Esch: S. 23, 28 – 39, 80 – 91, 154

ISBN 978-3-9816673-2-5